Map Workbook for

World History

Volume II: Since 1500

MAP WORKBOOK FOR

WORLD HISTORY

VOLUME II: SINCE 1500

PREPARED BY
CYNTHIA KOSSO
NORTHERN ARIZONA UNIVERSITY

West/Wadsworth
I(T)P® An International Thomson Publishing Company

Belmont, CA • Albany, NY • Bonn • Boston • Cincinnati • Detroit • Johannesburg • London
Madrid • Melbourne • Mexico City • New York • Paris • Singapore • Tokyo • Toronto • Washington

Printed in the United States of America
1 2 3 4 5 6 7 8 9 10

For more information, contact Wadsworth Publishing Company, 10 Davis Drive, Belmont, CA 94002, or electronically at http://www.thomson.com/wadsworth.html

International Thomson Publishing Europe
Berkshire House 168-173
High Holborn
London, WC1V 7AA, England

Thomas Nelson Australia
102 Dodds Street
South Melbourne 3205
Victoria, Australia

Nelson Canada
1120 Birchmount Road
Scarborough, Ontario
Canada M1K 5G4

International Thomson Publishing GmbH
Königswinterer Strasse 418
53227 Bonn, Germany

International Thomson Editores
Campos Eliseos 385, Piso 7
Col. Polanco
11560 México D.F. México

International Thomson Publishing Asia
221 Henderson Road
#05-10 Henderson Building
Singapore 0315

International Thomson Publishing Japan
Hirakawacho Kyowa Building, 3F
2-2-1 Hirakawacho
Chiyoda-ku, Tokyo 102, Japan

International Thomson Publishing Southern Africa
Building 18, Constantia Park
240 Old Pretoria Road
Halfway House, 1685 South Africa

Senior Developmental Editor: Sharon Adams Poore
Print Buyer: Stacey Weinberger

ISBN 0-534-53127-X

Volume Two
TABLE OF CONTENTS

INTRODUCTION

The creation of maps has a complex and evolving history. It is a very ancient human activity -- the oldest known map, from ca. 5000 BCE, was found in central Italy carved on a rock overlooking a Neolithic settlement. Another of our earliest existing maps is from the Babylonians in the fifth century BCE. In this map the Babylonians are situated precisely in the middle of the universe, and everything from them. Their own, and particularly the map maker's, perception of the world. As the Babylonian map suggests, a human viewpoint as an element in map making is common. [1]

Maps tell us about the physical and cultural aspects of the world, but they can be deceiving. Every map has a point of view or perspective. It has an author (the cartographer), a subject, and a theme. The subject and theme represent the author's interest, but also his or her skills, knowledge of geography, political viewpoints, and historical context. All map makers, therefore, pick a perspective from which to display their particular purpose or orientation, which occasionally is an intentionally false one. Colors, for example, can be and have been used subtly to suggest "good guys" or "bad guys." Countries can be drawn smaller or larger to suggest relative importance. To confuse an "enemy," the map maker may include incorrect details. A world map from the 16th century will show the continents as far as they were known to the Europeans during this age of discovery, but not as we believe them to be today. Any later chart of the Americas will depict the continent as very different in size and shape (clearly, the continents themselves did not change that much). Again, a world map reveals many things about its authors through the selection of details and perspective. In even the most "objective" map, however, one simply cannot add all details in all maps. The map would be rendered incomprehensibly complicated. Thus, it is good to keep in mind that maps do not represent reality, but a version of reality. Maps are like snapshots of the world, a moment in time and space with a definite historical context.

Despite these limitations, there are several basic principles governing the structure and reading of maps, and map reading remains an important part of any person's basic knowledge about the world, whether for travel or keeping track of events around the world. When someone gives you directions, or asks them of you, your brain automatically

---

[1]I would like to thank the undergraduate students, and in particular Clyde Wilson, in the History of Western Civilization courses at Northern Arizona University. They provided indispensable help and advice in the development of this workbook.

attempts to draw a rudimentary map. Your mind may even see roads as lines and rivers as bands or buildings as small squares.

To understand the basic appearance of a map, imagine the world as you see it from an airplane. The very straight lines that you see are generally roads and highways. The winding bands are rivers. Rectangles may be buildings and large dark green masses are forests. Cities are conglomerations of rectangles. If you simply took a picture from your airplane and had it printed you would have a photographic map: a reduced representation of a portion of the surface of the earth. How we see the world from an airplane is, however, somewhat different from how we see it on a map. The world is round. The map page is flat. All map makers, therefore, pick a perspective (as we have seen) and a scale from which to display their particular purpose or orientation.

Since the world is round and most maps are not there is also an unavoidable distortion is the spatial representation of locations. (You may notice that the shapes of continents change slightly from map to map. This is because the distortion is different depending upon the perspective of the map.) Flat maps, however, are not likely to be completely superseded by globes. Carrying a globe on a hike or road trip would be very inconvenient.

In order to make a map (or to read one) a frame of reference is chosen. A grid system within the frame of reference is usually used to help pinpoint locations on the map. In this exercise book, the grid pattern has been removed in order to make the maps less cluttered, but normally the lines of latitude and longitude would be included on the map. These lines appear on most maps you might consult.

Map makers, in order to build a grid system, chose the north and south poles as two definite points from which to begin dividing the world. Midway between these poles a line was drawn around the world (this is the equator). The lines of latitude run parallel to the equator up and down to each pole. The equator provides a natural line from which to measure, but there is no such natural longitude line (but one is put in by convention and is called the prime meridian). A longitudinal starting point is obviously needed as a point of reference. Lines of longitude complete the grid by drawing lines from pole to pole around the planet (the standard one passing through Greenwich, England for historical reasons -- now the commonly accepted prime meridian).

The longitudinal line through Greenwich, England is now used as an accepted reference point, but many nations have, in the past, created maps with their own most important cities as reference points. The United States made maps with Washington DC as the prime meridian. Spain drew it through Madrid, the Greeks through Athens, the Dutch through Amsterdam and so on.

Many different scales of maps are also used. That simply means that there are maps with different proportions between the distance on the map and the actual distance on the world. The larger the fraction (or proportion), the smaller the territory covered. Inches per mile or centimeters per kilometer are the most common kind of scale. The scale is merely a fraction comparing the distances on the map measured in inches or centimeters, with the distances on the ground measured in miles or kilometers (e.g., 1 inch on the map = 10 miles on the ground).

Although the entire process insures that maps will always represent a version of reality, instead of reality itself, maps are becoming more and more accurate. [2] Cartographers have worked to perfect maps since the late middle ages, with much success. This success is our gain, as it enhances our understanding of history, geography, meteorology, cultural and economic distributions of people, ... the list is endless.

That is precisely the purpose of this exercise book -- to help you learn to read and understand maps as well as to help you understand the relation between places and people through time. The maps will help you order events and historical locations. Nearly all exercises incorporate three parts. There is a brief introduction to each exercise. The section marked "locations" asks you to find and correctly place on the map provided cities, boundaries and other features. The "questions" section asks you to attempt to relate, or synthesize, the historical and geographical information that you have absorbed.

BRIEF BIBLIOGRAPHY

Demko, George with Jerome Agel and Eugene Boe. 1992. *Why in the World, Adventures in Geography*. New York: Doubleday. This is a fun and easy to read introduction to mapping and geography. It does an excellent job of pointing out the importance of geography.

Greenhood, David. 1964. *Mapping*. Chicago: University of Chicago Press. This book provides a clear and concise introduction to maps and mapping.

Wood, Denis. 1992. *The Power of Maps*. New York: The Guilford Press. In this book Wood shows how maps are used and abused. It is an excellent introduction to the way maps have been used by groups and individuals to make an argument or present a point of view.

---

[2]The new, 1993, Hammond, Atlas of the World, is a beautiful example of this trend.

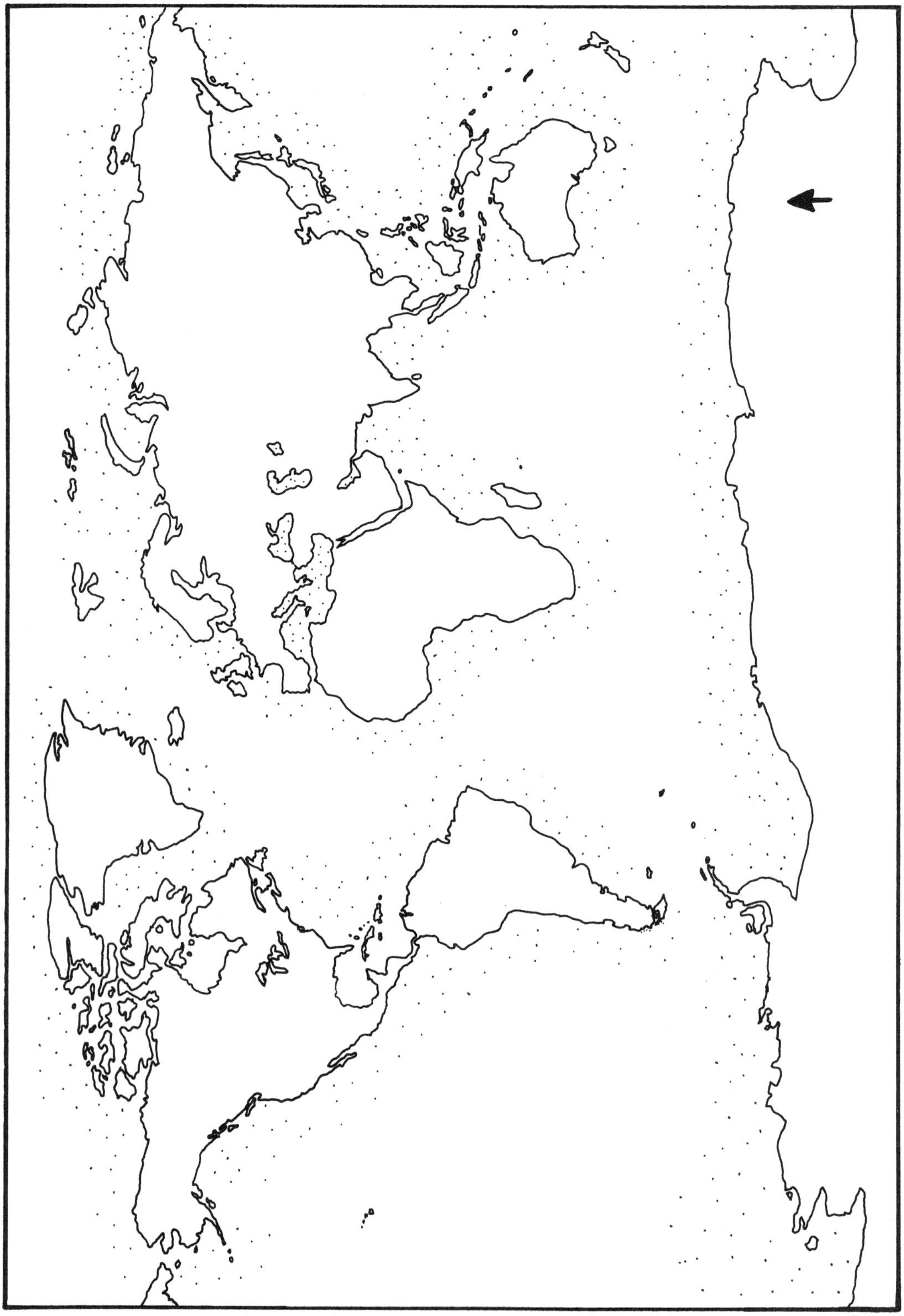

Exercise 1
The World: Major Regions

Introduction

This exercise puts into perspective the major regions of the planet, as we know them today. Civilizations developed in a world context. They were not, and are not, isolated entities. Interactions among the various regions and people are evident from very early in human history. People traded with one another for food, tools and raw materials. In that process, they learned about one another, sometimes adopting practices, sometimes improving upon the technologies and customs that they found.

The earliest civilizations were found worldwide, in the hills and valleys of Mesoamerica, the Fertile Crescent, India, China and Egypt.

Locations

With different colored pencils, shade or draw in and number the following regions and geographical features. You may number the locations and place the numbers on the map for clarity.

A. Regions

1. Anatolia
2. Arabia
3. Australia
4. Balkan Peninsula
5. Britain
6. China
7. Egypt
8. Fertile Crescent
9. Iberian Peninsula
10. Iran
11. Japan
12. North Africa
13. North America
14. Russia
15. South America
16. Southeast Asia

B. Rivers

17. Amazon
18. Danube
19. Ganges
20. Mississippi
21. Nile
22. Rhine
23. Tigris
24. Yangtze

C. Seas, Oceans, Lakes

25. Atlantic Ocean
26. Black Sea
27. Caribbean
28. Great Lakes
29. Indian Ocean
30. Mediterranean
31. North Sea
32. Pacific Ocean
33. Persian Gulf
34. Red Sea

D. Mountains

35. Alps
36. Caucasus
37. Himalayan Mts.
38. Pyrennes
39. Rockies
40. Taurus

Questions

In some ways, the development of civilizations remains a mystery. What are some of the theories used to explain their existence? What advantages and disadvantages do civilizations offer to us as human beings?

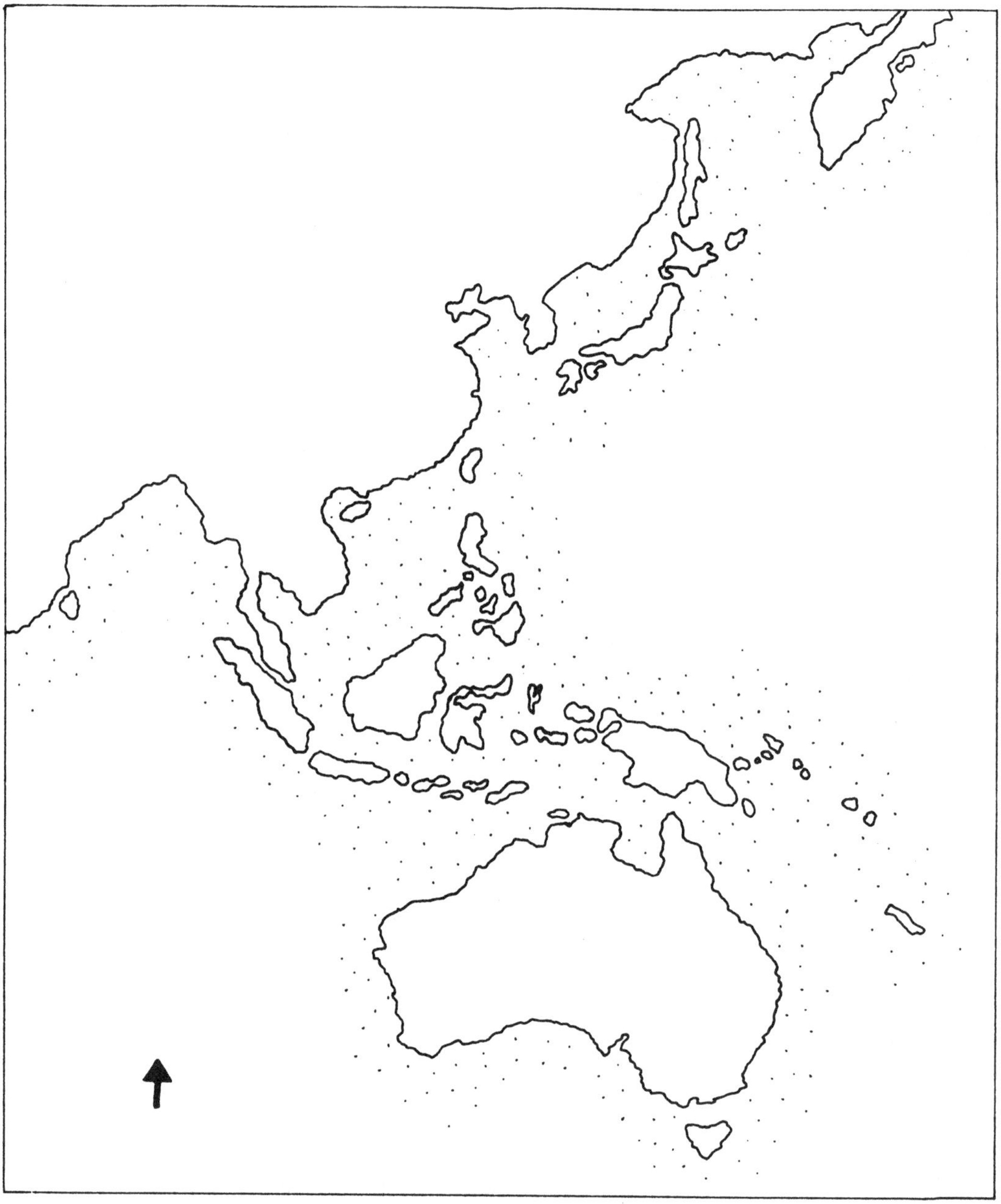

Exercise 2
Southeast Asia

Introduction

Few westerners know much about Southeast Asia, beyond the fact that the Vietnam war was fought in the region. This region was, however, home to one of the world's earliest bronze-age societies (in northern Thailand). Rice cultivation appeared perhaps as early as 9,000 years before the modern era.

There is an immense number of races, cultures, and religions in this part of Asia. This mixture is emphasized and increased because the region serves as a link between China, India and the islands of the South Pacific. For example, early in its history, the state of Srivijaya played a major role in commercial contact between China and India. Moreover the region quickly became integrated into global markets after the arrival of the Europeans This exercise introduces you to just a few of the cities and regions in Southeast Asia.

Locations

With different colored pencils, shade in and label the following cities or settlements and regions.

A. Cities

1. Batavia
2. Canton
3. Indrapura
4. Macao
5. Madras
6. Malacca
7. Manila

B. Regions

8. Angkor
9. Borneo
10. Champa
11. Mlaya
12. Nan Chao
13. Philippines
14. Srivijaya
15. Sumatra

Questions

Using a description of the geographical environment of the region, explain why Southeast Asia was never unified under a single government. What trade goods were most important to the economies of the region?

Exercise 3
European Conquests and Possessions in the West Indies

Introduction

In 1492 a new era in world history was launched. European adventurers took their ships in search of wealth, fame and new worlds to conquer and convert. These men provoked a transformation of Africa, Asia, the America's and Europe itself. This exercise looks at just one small part of the world affected by the European voyages and conquests.

Locations

With different colored pencils, shade in and number the following islands or regions and European spheres of influence.

A. Islands or regions

1. Bahamas
2. Belize
3. Cuba
4. Florida
5. Jamaica
6. Lesser Antilles
7. Mosquito Coast
8. Puerto Rico

B. Spheres of influence

9. English areas
10. Spanish areas

Questions

What motivated European settlement in the West Indies? Discuss the short and long term impact of European settlement on the people and environment of the West Indies. What impact did the discovery of the West Indies have on the countries and people of Europe?

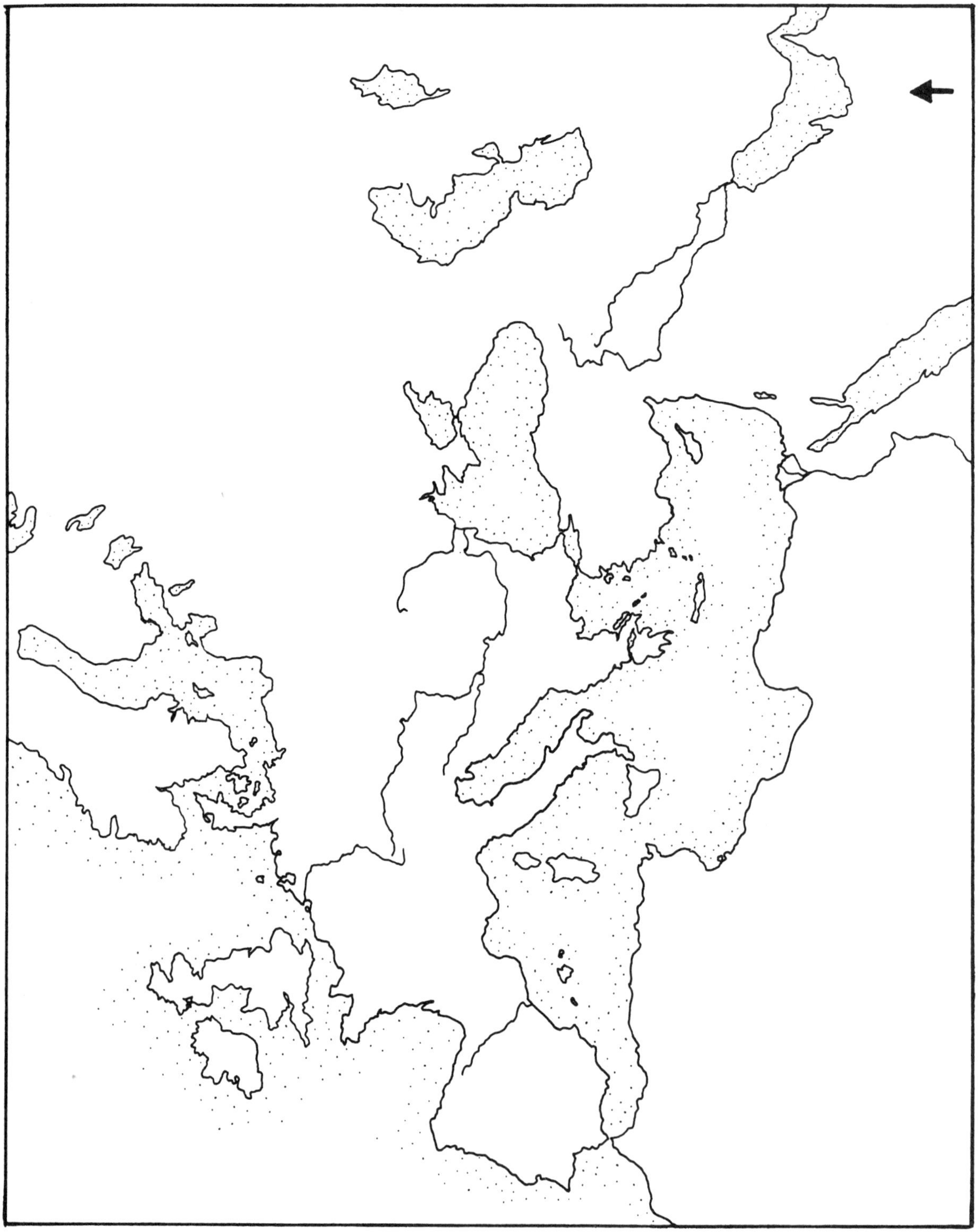

Exercise 4
Catholics and Protestants: 1550 AD

Introduction

In the sixteenth century abuses by the Catholic church, in particular the Papacy, were reaching a crisis point. Many reform movements grew out of the frustration of the times, some made surprisingly influential by the dissemination of these new ideas through the written word, now easily spread because of the printing press. The Reformation in Germany was to be one of the most influential. This particular reform movement was led by Martin Luther, the founder of Lutheranism. It was not long before the population of Europe had chosen sides: Protestant (e.g. Lutheran, Calvinist, Anglican) or Catholic. This exercise identifies some of the divisions, by religion, that appeared by the mid sixteenth century.

Locations

On your map, number the following cites and countries. Next to each number, write in the local religion (e.g. 1 - Roman Catholic).

A. Cities

1. Dijon
2. Dublin
3. Edinburgh
4. Lisbon
5. London
6. Munich
7. Paris
8. Rome
9. Seville
10. Trent

B. Countries

11. Denmark
12. Netherlands
13. Norway
14. Poland
15. Sweden

Questions

Compare and contrast the Reformation in England and Germany. Were the same reforming factors at work? Who initiated the Reformation in England? In Germany?

What impact did the Reformation have on society in Europe? Give several examples.

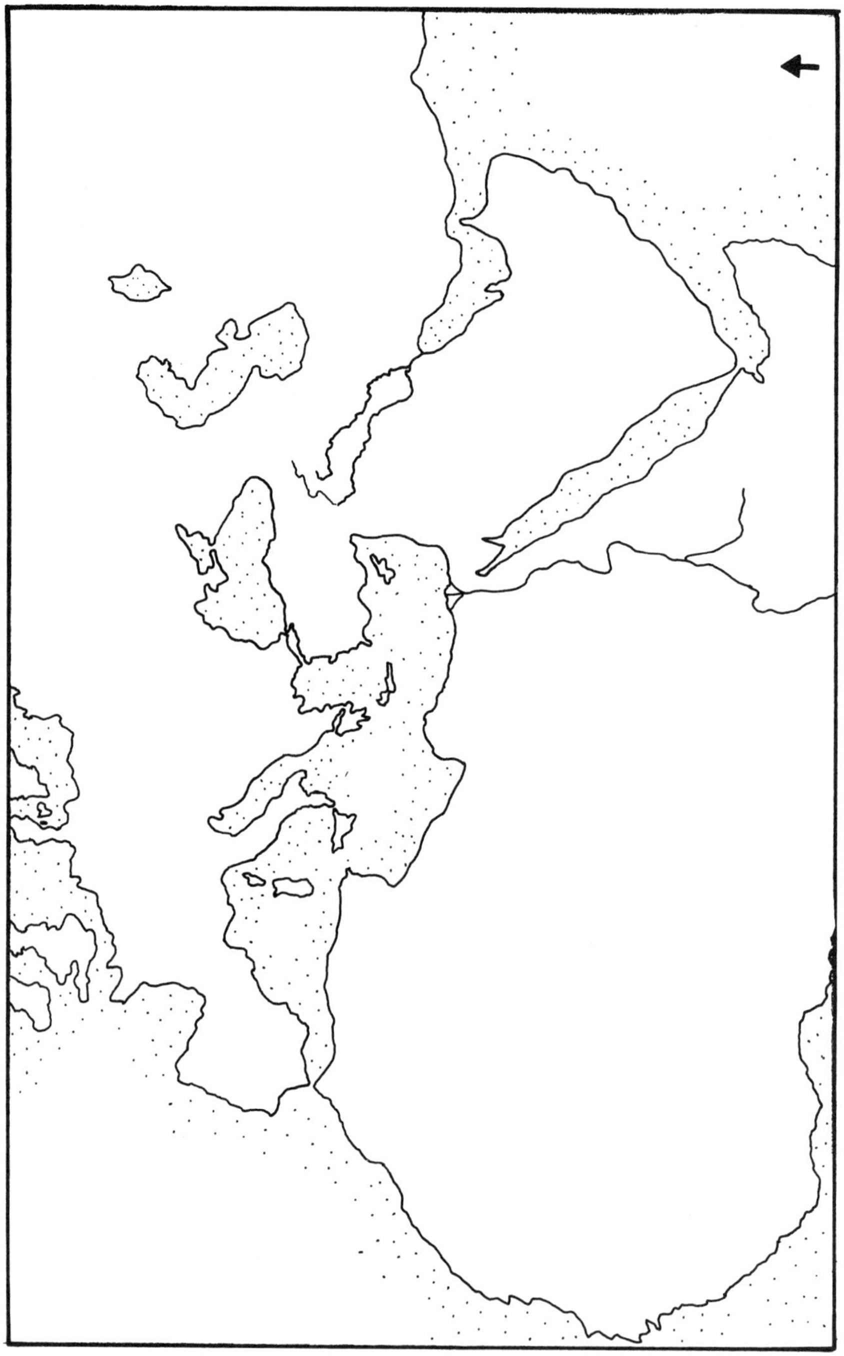

Exercise 5
The Turks and Their Neighbors

Introduction

Muslim empires dominated the Middle East and South Asia for several centuries. Despite European pressure, they brought stability to a traditionally unsettled region until the eighteenth century. By the end of the eighteenth century the powerful Ottoman Empire of the Turks had gradually begun to decline in power.

This exercise introduces you to the Middle East.

Locations

With different colored pencils, number the following cities, people, regions and geographical features and shade in the following imperial boundaries.

A. Cities

1. Aleppo
2. Damascus
3. Isfahan
4. Istanbul
5. Salonica
6. Tabriz

B. People

7. Circassians
8. Uzbeks

C. Regions and geographical features

9. Aral Sea
10. Black Sea
11. Caspian Sea
12. Crimea
13. Euphrates River
14. Georgia
15. Mediterranean Sea
16. Morea
17. Najd
18. Persian Gulf

D. Boundaries

19. Ottoman empire (at its height)
20. Safavid empire (at its height)

Questions

What factors allowed the Ottomans to overthrow the Byzantine Empire in the 15th century? What factors finally limited the expansion of the Ottoman Empire into the Balkans? What are the main differences and similarities among the Moslem empires discussed in chapter 18?

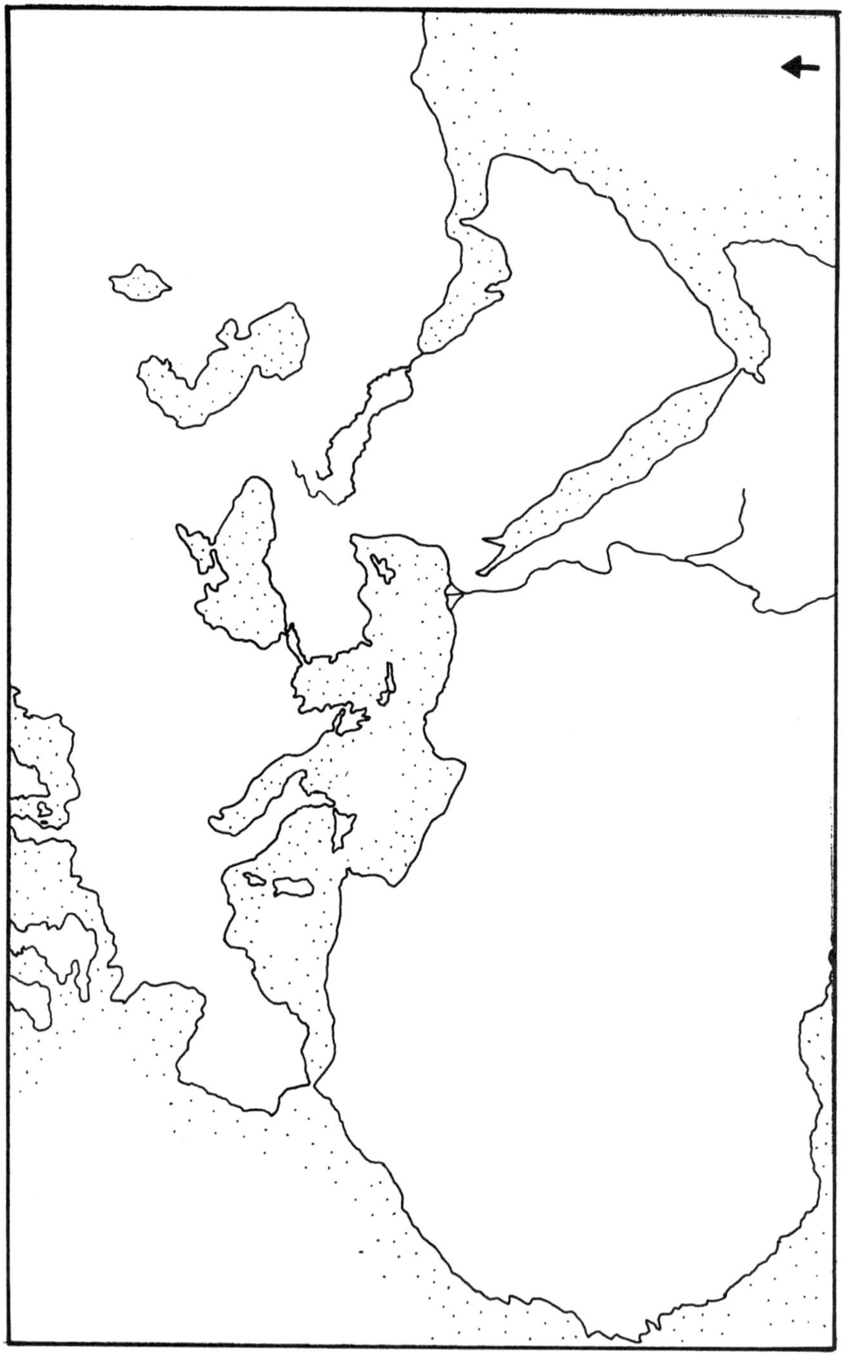

Exercise 6
The Ottoman Empire

Introduction

The Turkish people, led by the Ottomans, conquered the Byzantine Empire once and for all in 1453 with the capture of Constantinople. This was a tremendous victory and afterwards the Turks were on the move. They added vast tracts of lands to their wealthy empire.

The Ottomans were very effective at getting the Europeans to accept them as an equal power. They had a very intricate and effective government, with a strong and well organized military. This exercise traces the growth of Ottoman strength and influence in Europe and the Mediterranean regions.

Locations

With different colored pencils trace the boundaries of the Ottoman empire and locate the following regions and cities on your map.

A. Boundaries of the Ottoman empire

1. 1451
2. 1481
3. 1521
4. 1566

B. Regions

5. Anatolia
6. Egypt
7. Syria
8. Transylvania
9. Wallachia

C. Cities

10. Cairo
11. Athens
12. Belgrade
13. Damascus
14. Istanbul
15. Tunis

Questions

After 1566 the northern boundaries of the Ottoman empire were fairly fixed. What occurred to stop further movement in that direction? What were the strengths and weaknesses of the Ottomans? What were the long term results of their conquests?

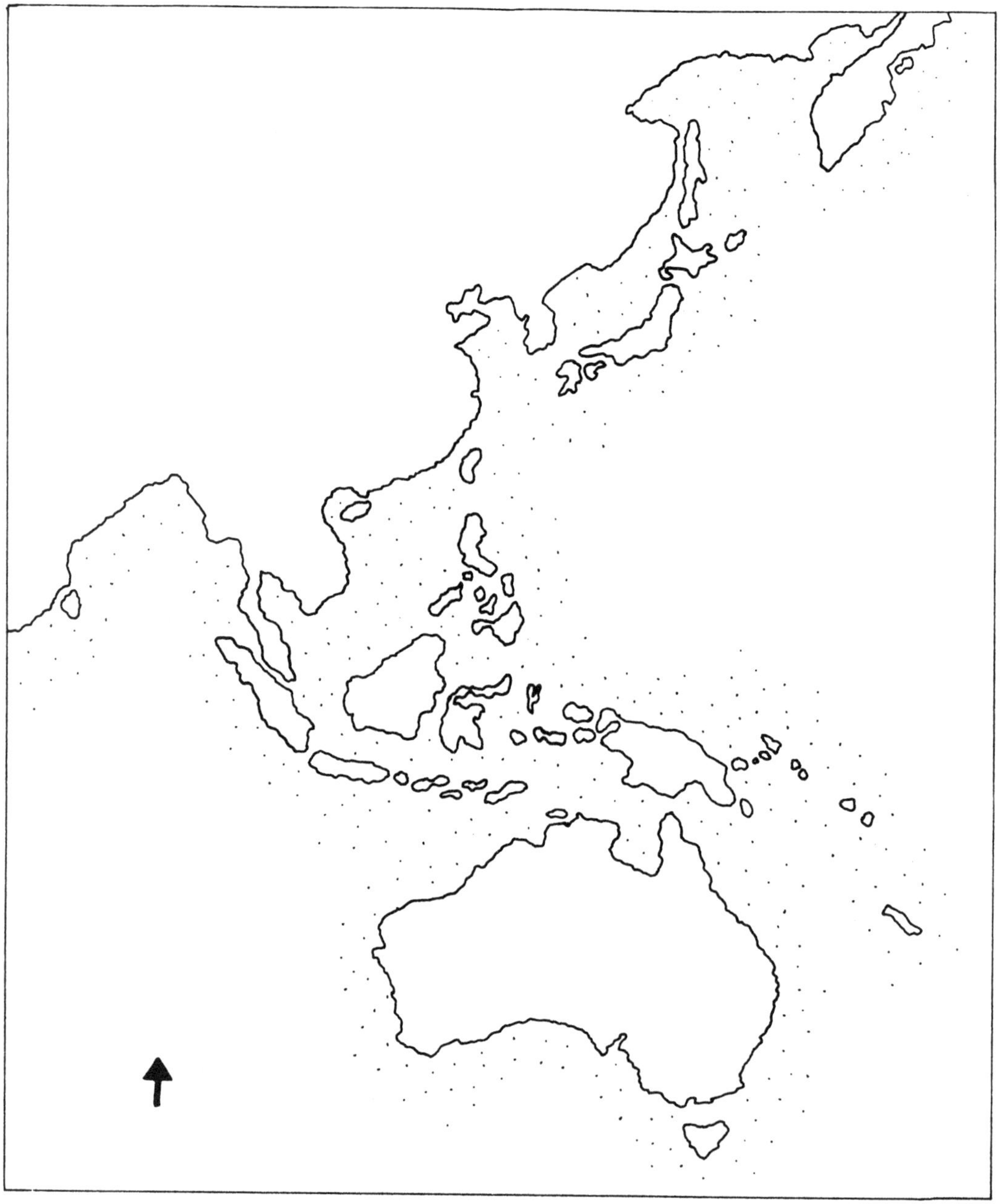

Exercise 7
East Asia: 1500-1800

Introduction

Vital new societies continued to develop in East Asia. Chinese and Japanese cultures earned the admiration and envy of neighbors and European observers. When the Portuguese first encountered the Chinese, this eastern civilization was the most advanced on earth.

In Japan, the 15th century ushered in an era of rivalries, but by the mid-16th century a process of unification had begun. Once in power, the dominant Tokugawa rulers initiated a long period of peace. This allowed economic growth and the flowering of Japanese cultural arts, such as literature, drama, pottery and painting.

Locations

With different colored pencils, place on your map the numbers of the following cities, then number and lightly shade in the regions and states.

A. Cities

1. Asano
2. Beijing
3. Canton
4. Changsha
5. Hosokawa
6. Kuroda
7. Nanjing
8. Sakai
9. Todo
10. Tsugaru
11. Wuhan

B. Regions and states

12. Burma
13. Cambodia
14. Guandong
15. Hunan
16. Inner Mongolia
17. Manchuria
18. Sichuan
19. Taiwan
20. Vietnam

Questions

Describe the factors that led to the decline and fall of the Ming dynasty. Who were the Qing and how did they consolidate their power? List the states that participated in the tributary system of the Qing. What factors led to their incorporation into the system? Were they willing or unwilling participants?

What motivated the Japanese to isolate themselves from western cultures? Were they able to succeed?

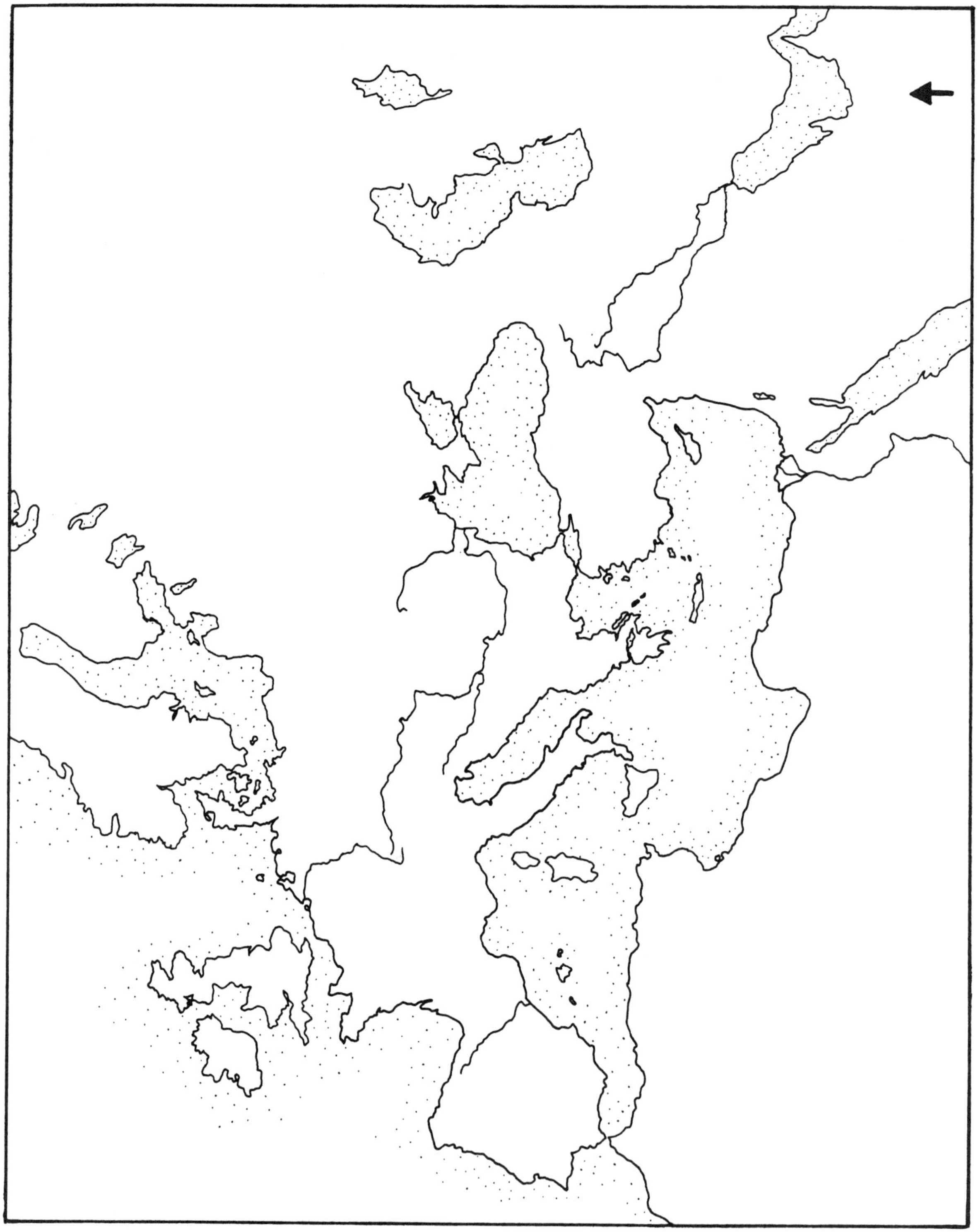

Exercise 8
The Enlightenment

Introduction

Because of the vast changes in communications, particularly the creation of the printing press, new ideas and trends spread faster than ever before. In the 18th century, four intellectual developments merged and were disseminated to create the revolutionary movement known as the Enlightenment. This exercise introduces you to some of the academic centers that were integral to the creation of the Enlightenment.

Locations

With different colored pencils locate the following centers of learning and publication.

A. Universities

1. Cambridge
2. Gottingen
3. Leiden

B. Publication sites

4. Amsterdam
5. Berlin
6. Florence
7. Geneva
8. London
9. Rome

C. Academic centers

10. Bologna
11. Copenhagen
12. Madrid
13. Turin
14. Uppsala
15. Venice

Questions

Describe the nature of the four intellectual developments. Name and discuss at least one important proponent of each of these.

What impact did the Enlightenment have on the debate about the nature and value of women? Who made the strongest case for the rights of women and what did this author write?

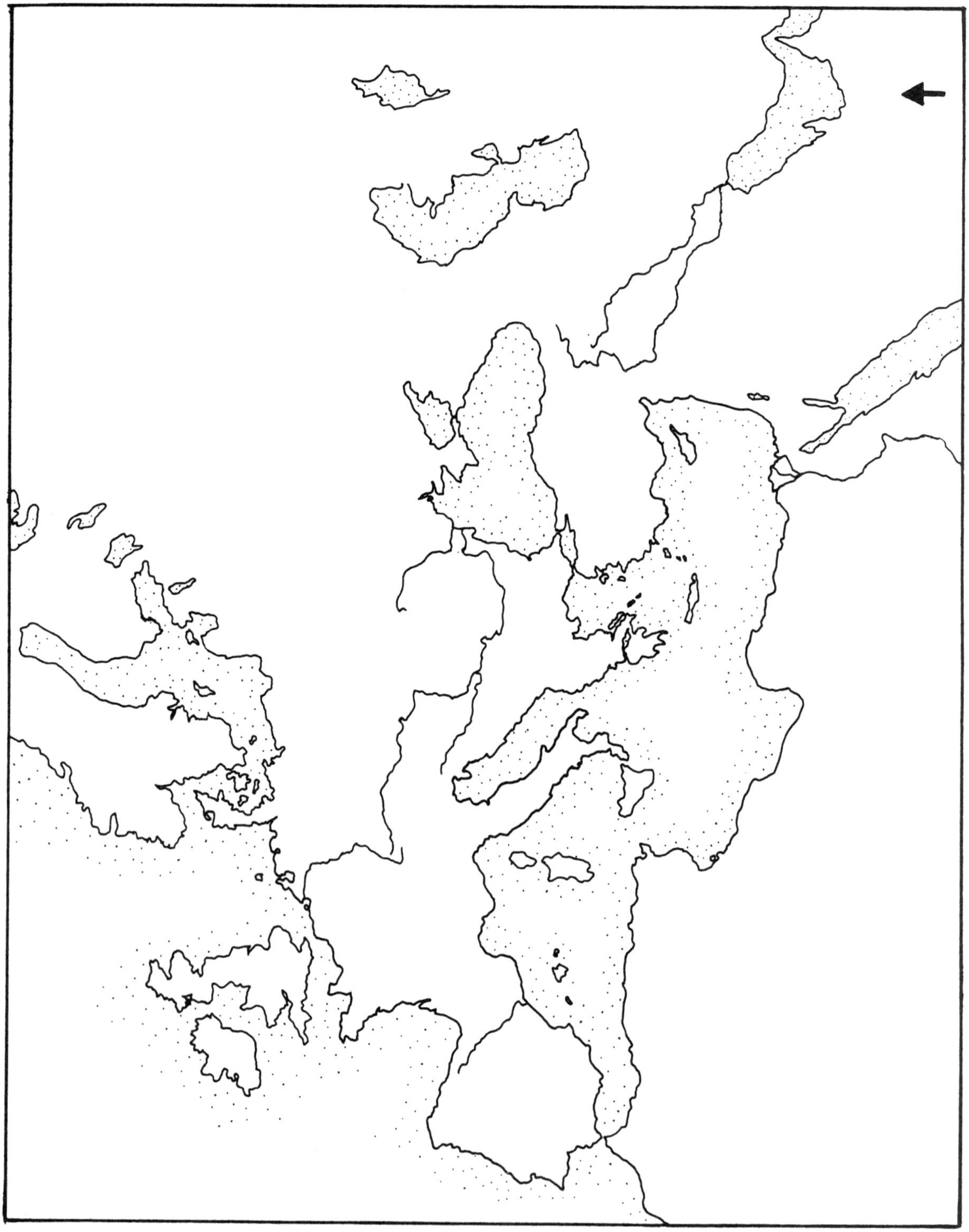

Exercise 9
Napoleon's Empire

Introduction

The late eighteenth century saw two important revolutions in the west: the American revolution and the French revolution. Both were the result of long term problems. The French sought, like the Americans, to ground their constitution in the idea of equal rights. The implementation of equal rights was neither easy nor peaceful. Other European nations feared that violent upheaval would spread from France and, thus, an informal coalition formed against the French. In response, the French had built up a large and impressive army and conquered even the Netherlands. Terror, instability and confusion soon dominated French politics and the economy. This situation allowed Napoleon to stage the coup d'état that would bring him to power. With his power he would try to create a long-lasting European empire, enlightened and fair. This exercise traces the growth of the Napoleonic state in Europe.

Locations

With a colored pencil outline the boundaries of the French Empire under Napoleon then outline the boundaries of and place the number of the following neighboring territories. Next to the number, place the status of the territory with respect to the French Empire (e.g., allied).

A. French Empire under Napoleon
1. Confederacy of the Rhineland
2. Corsica
3. Grand Duchy of Warsaw
4. Imperial boundaries
5. Kingdom of Italy
6. Kingdom of Naples
7. Kingdom of Sicily
8. Sardinia
9. Saxony
10. Spain

Questions

What lands were gained by Napoleon? His was not a long lived empire. Why not? What factors ultimately led to his downfall?

Generally what were the results of the revolutions of the eighteenth century? What were some of the major social, political, and territorial changes?

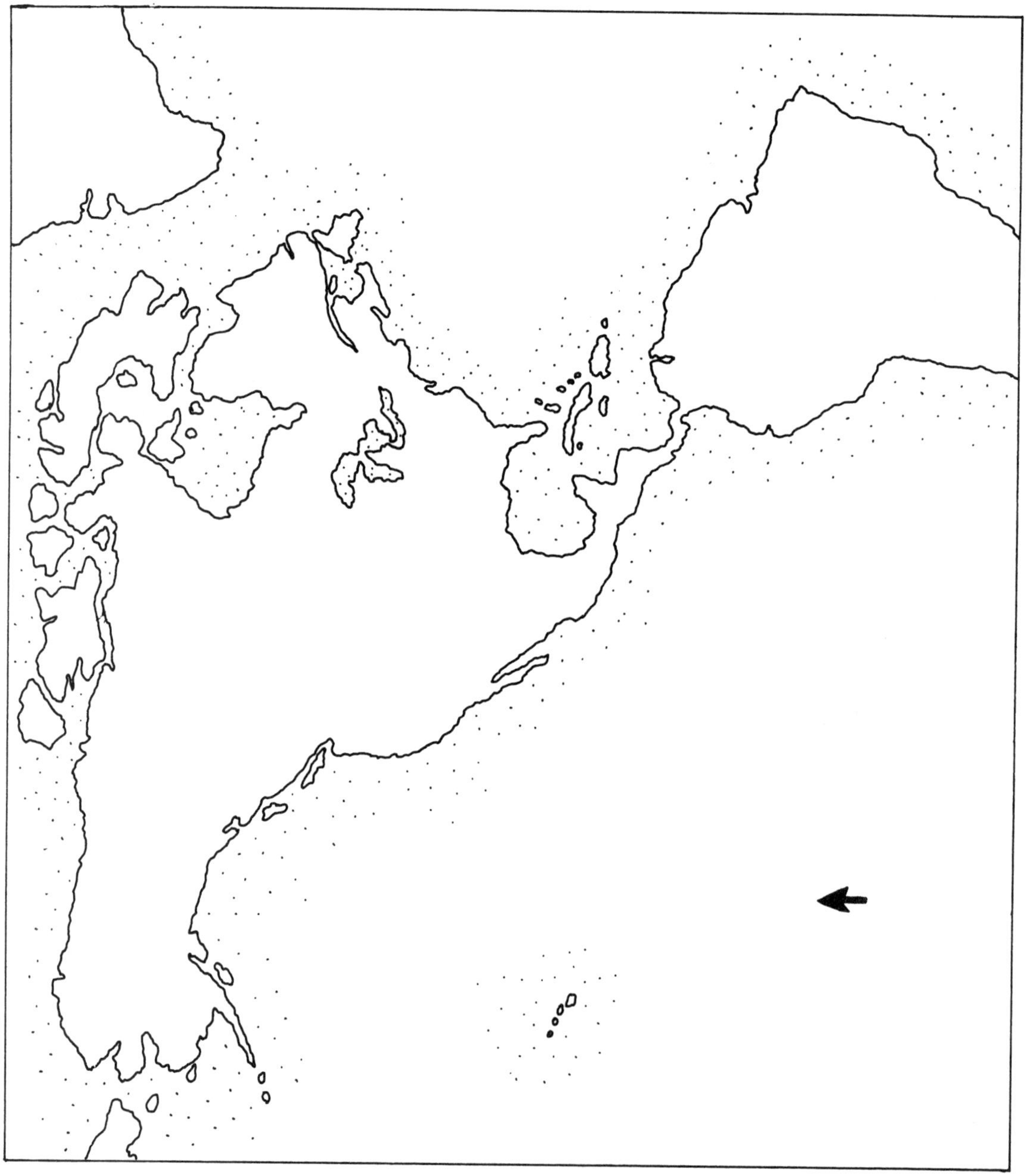

Exercise 10
Colonization and Independence in North America

Introduction

With the discovery of the Americas by the Europeans, a new era was begun. European powers claimed these territories for themselves, regardless of the original inhabitant's desires. Europeans brought with them a new way of life and old conflicts. It has taken hundreds of years to begin to sort out these conflicts fought on American soil.

This exercise introduces you to the European territories of North America.

Locations

On the map provided lightly shade in and number, using different colors, the following areas of European influences, control and colonies (by the 18th century), North American boundaries and the following cities and geographical features.

A. European influences, control and colonies

1. Dutch
2. English
3. French
4. Spanish

B. Boundaries

5. USA in 1803
6. USA in 1848
7. Canada in 1867
8. Canada in 1912

C. Cities

9. Boston
10. Chicago
11. Denver
12. New Orleans
13. New York
14. Philadelphia
15. Quebec
16. San Francisco
17. Vancouver
18. Washington DC
19. Winnipeg

D. Geographical features

20. Colorado River
21. Great Lakes
22. Hudson Bay
23. Mississippi River
24. Missouri River
25. Rocky Mts.

Questions

In general, what happened to the societies found in North America by the European powers? How did the shifting boundaries, in particular, impact the native inhabitants? What explains European military successes over these societies?

By what means and for what reasons did the new USA free itself from British rule? How was this move similar and different from developments in Canada?

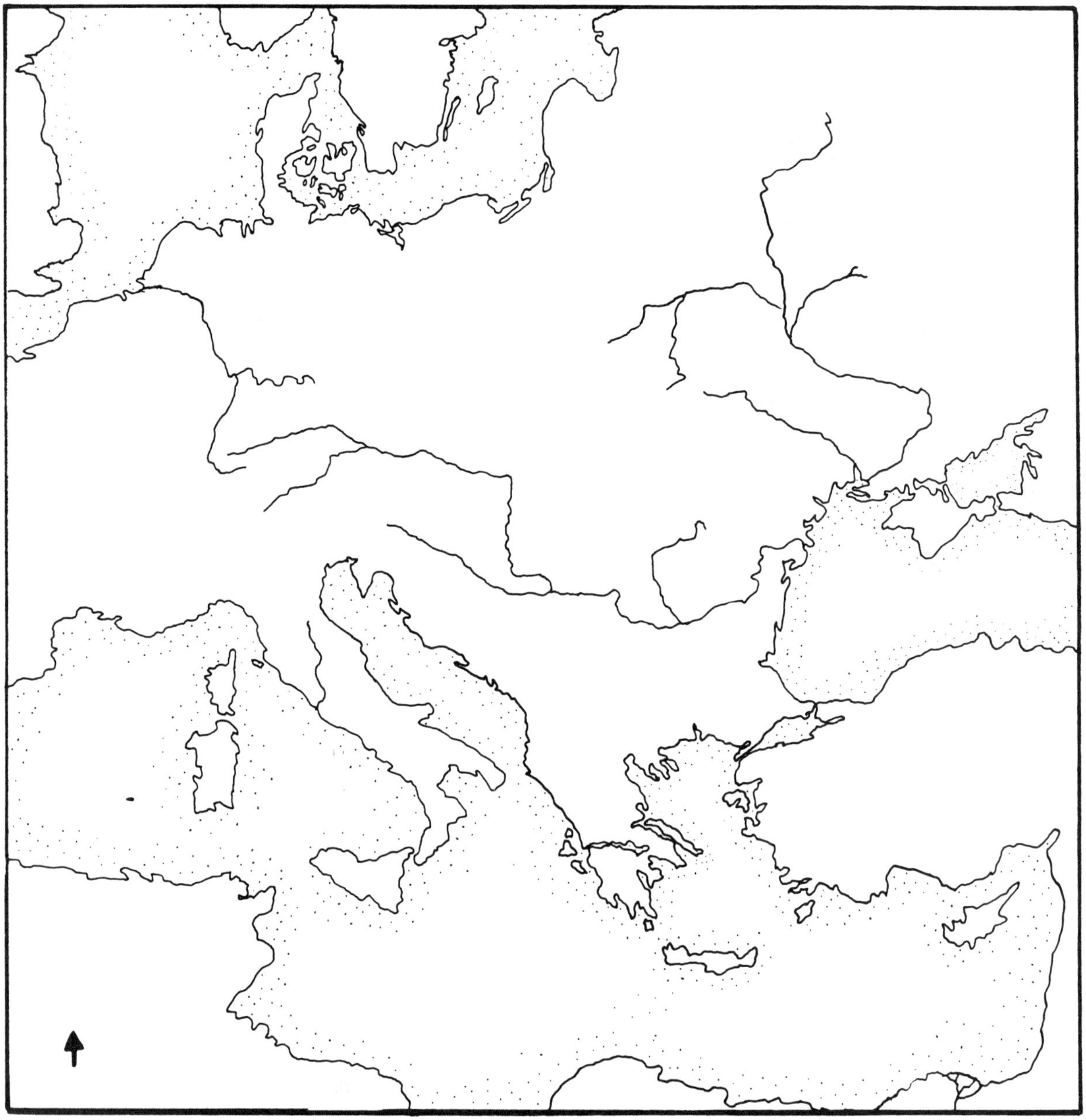

Exercise 11
The German States in the Eighteenth Century

Introduction

After the end of the Thirty-Years war, Germany was still made up of more than three hundred independent states. The Holy Roman Empire was an entity in name only. Out of the hundreds of German states, two became most powerful: Brandenburg and Austria. Both of these states would grow and strengthen because of particularly dominating families, the Hohenzollerns and the Hapsburgs respectively.

The boundaries and peoples of these regions of Europe were mobile and unstable. This exercise is intended to give you an idea for how these German and Slavic regions were defined.

Locations

With different colored marking pencils number, date, and draw the boundaries (with as much accuracy as possible) for the following Germanic, Austrian and Slavic states and regions. Also place the number of the following cities in their proper locations.

A. States
1. Austria
2. Bosnia
3. Bulgaria
4. Hungary
5. Poland
6. Prussia
7. Russian Empire
8. Serbia
9. Ukraine

B. Regions
10. Bavaria
11. Crimea
12. Prussia
13. Saxony

C. Cities
14. Belgrade
15. Berlin
16. Breslau
17. Budapest
18. Cracow
19. Dresden
20. Munich
21. Nuremberg
22. Prague
23. Venice
24. Vienna
25. Warsaw

Questions

What were the long term goals of the Hohenzollern dynasty? How successful were they in achieving their goals?

The Austrians had long been important. Describe the Austrian government. What factors made it develop as it did? Why did the Hapsburgs decide to move into more eastern territories and abandon the thought of a purely German empire?

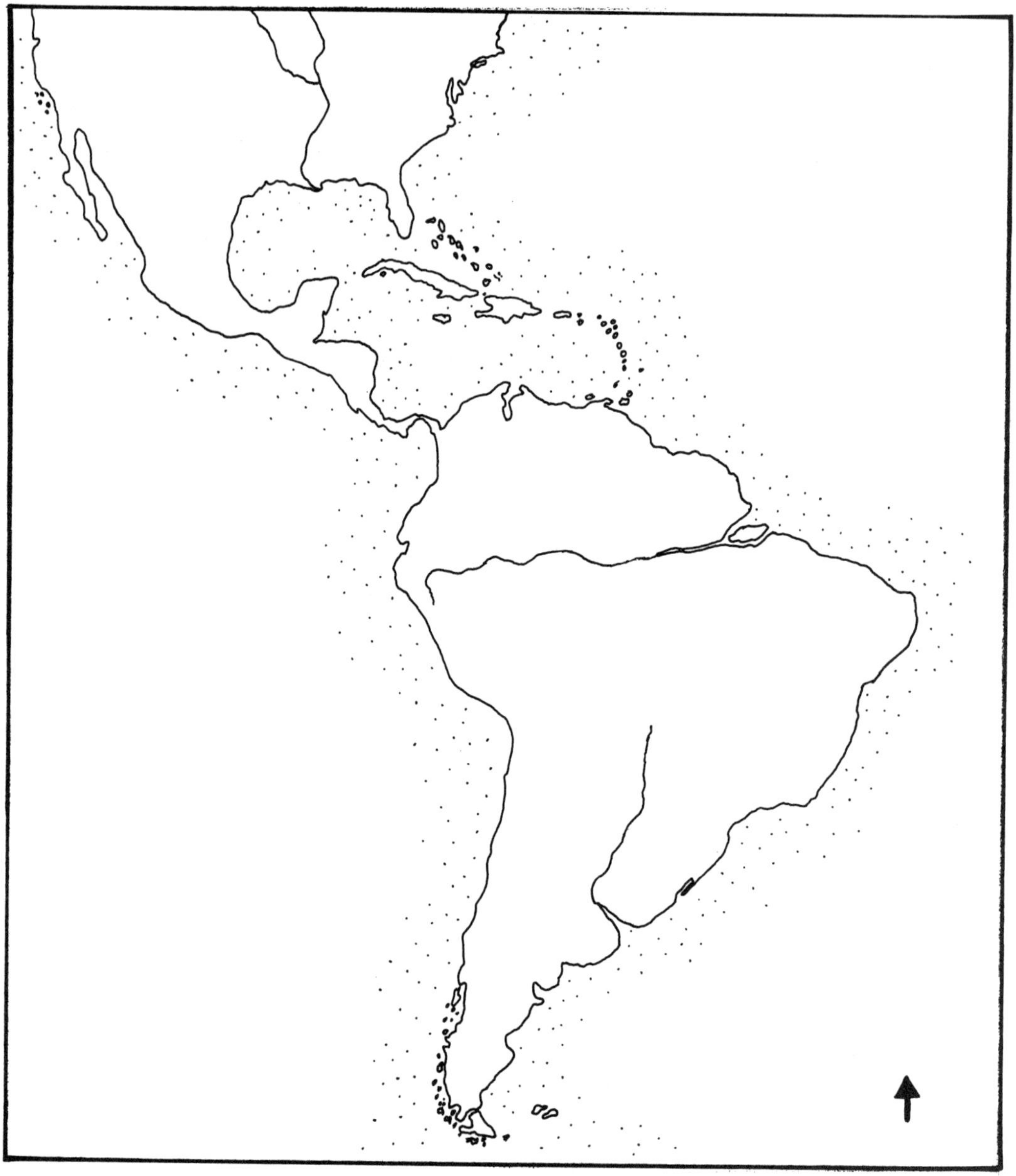

Exercise 12
Colonization and Independence in Central and South America

Introduction

Latin America holds a special fascination for those of us residing in North America. In politics the United States has felt the area to be of vital national interest and has thereby justified centuries of interference in the internal workings of national states. Yet despite this continual contact, as a group, North Americans have lacked understanding of their southern neighbors.

This exercise introduces you to some of the regions of Central and South America and shows you how recently most of these states have achieved independence.

Locations

With different colored marking pencils trace the boundaries of and number the following colonies, cities, and then trace the borders, number and write date of independence for the following independent states.

A. Colonies
1. English
2. French
3. Portuguese
4. Spanish

B. Cities
5. Bogotá
6. Caracas
7. Lima
8. Quito
9. Rio de Janeiro
10. Santa Fe
11. Sao Paulo

C. Independent states
12. Bolivia
13. Brazil
14. Chile
15. Colombia
16. Costa Rica
17. Ecuador
18. Haiti
19. Nicaragua
20. Peru

Questions

Which states most recently achieved independence? Which regions resisted colonization the longest, and why? What factors led to and encouraged the growth of the independence movement?

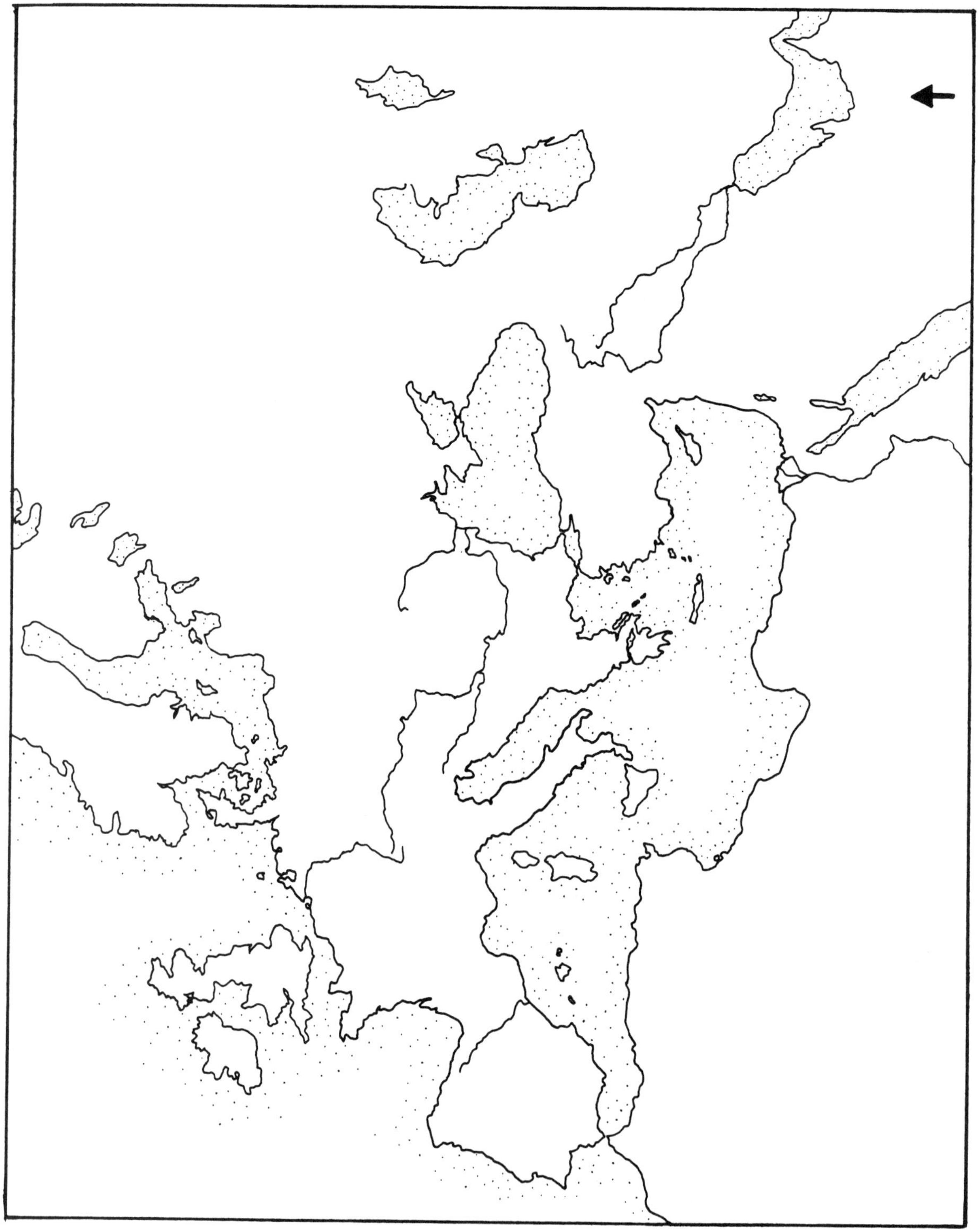

Exercise 13
Europe after the Congress of Vienna

Introduction

By 1815 a measure of territorial stability was restored to the European continent. In some case the old monarchies were also restored. Peace arrangements were made in an attempt to contain the forces for change unleashed in the late eighteenth century. Such attempts would prove to be futile in the long run. This exercise provides a familiarity with the nations of the early nineteenth century.

Locations

With colored marking pencils number and carefully draw the boundaries the following states.

1. Denmark
2. France
3. Germanic Confederation
4. Great Britain
5. Kingdom of the Two Sicilies
6. Netherlands
7. Papal States
8. Portugal
9. Spain
10. Switzerland

Questions

Briefly describe the problems that the conservative movement had in containing forces for change. What role did Metternich play in these conservative attempts to maintain order? Name three areas where there were revolts and describe the European response.

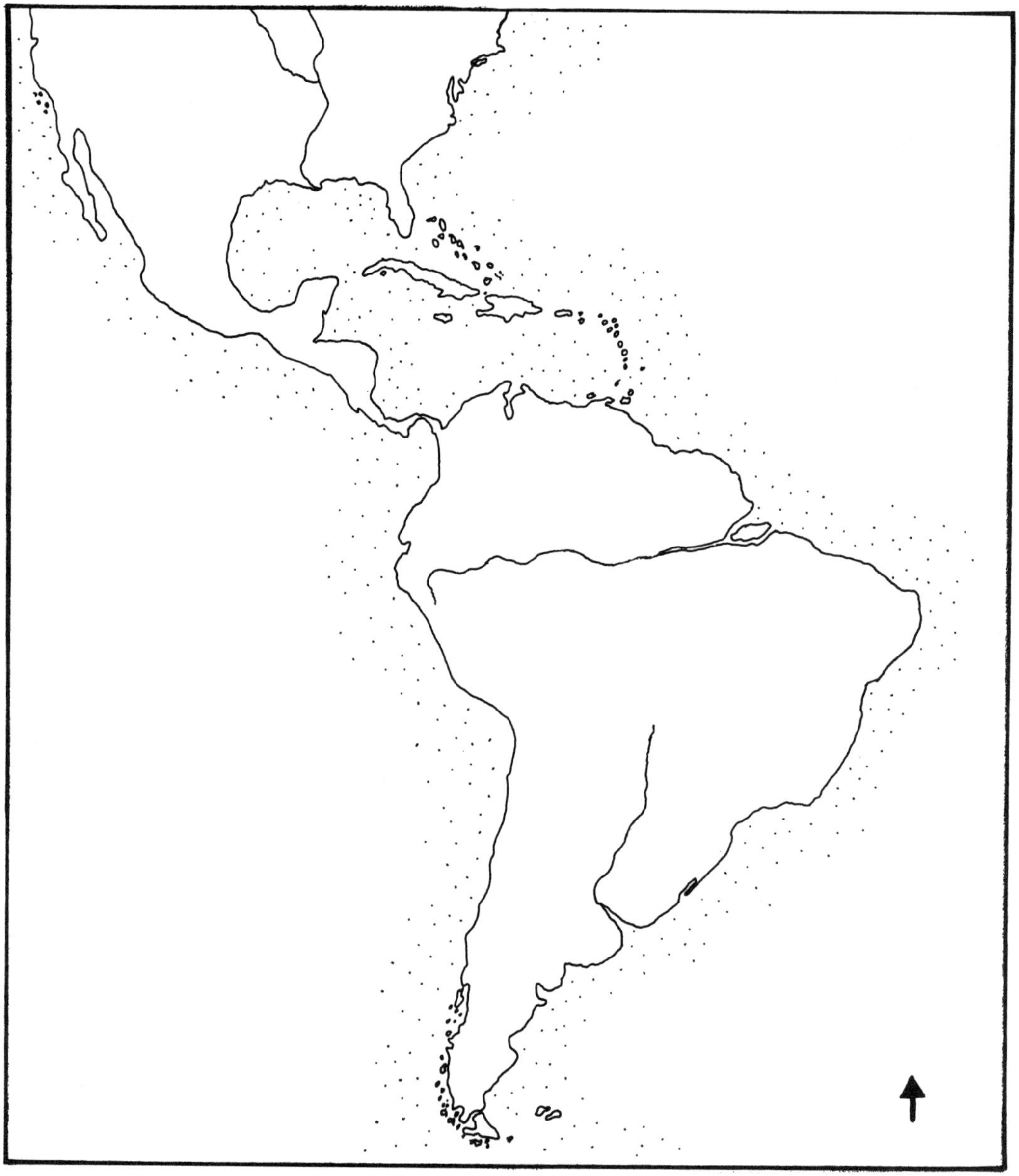

Exercise 14

Independent Nations of Latin America (1845)

Introduction

The revolutions that freed North America had little immediate effect on the colonial status of countries in South and Central America. These lands remained in the hands of colonial powers into the nineteenth century. The Spanish and the Portuguese held these territories and were loath to give up their wealth, even though their powers were weakening. Slowly the lands of South America demanded and got independence, despite Spanish use of well trained troops to quell the rebellions.

Locations

With a marking pencil number, draw the boundaries and provide the date of independence for the following nations of South and Central America.

1. Argentina
2. Bolivia
3. Brazil
4. Chile
5. Columbia
6. Costa Rica
7. Ecuador
8. El Salvador
9. Guatemala
10. Honduras
11. Nicaragua
12. Paraguay
13. Peru
14. Uruguay
15. Venezuela

Questions

Which Latin American states failed to gain their independence at this time (1845)? What role did the United States play in movement for independence in Latin America? Why did the United States become involved?

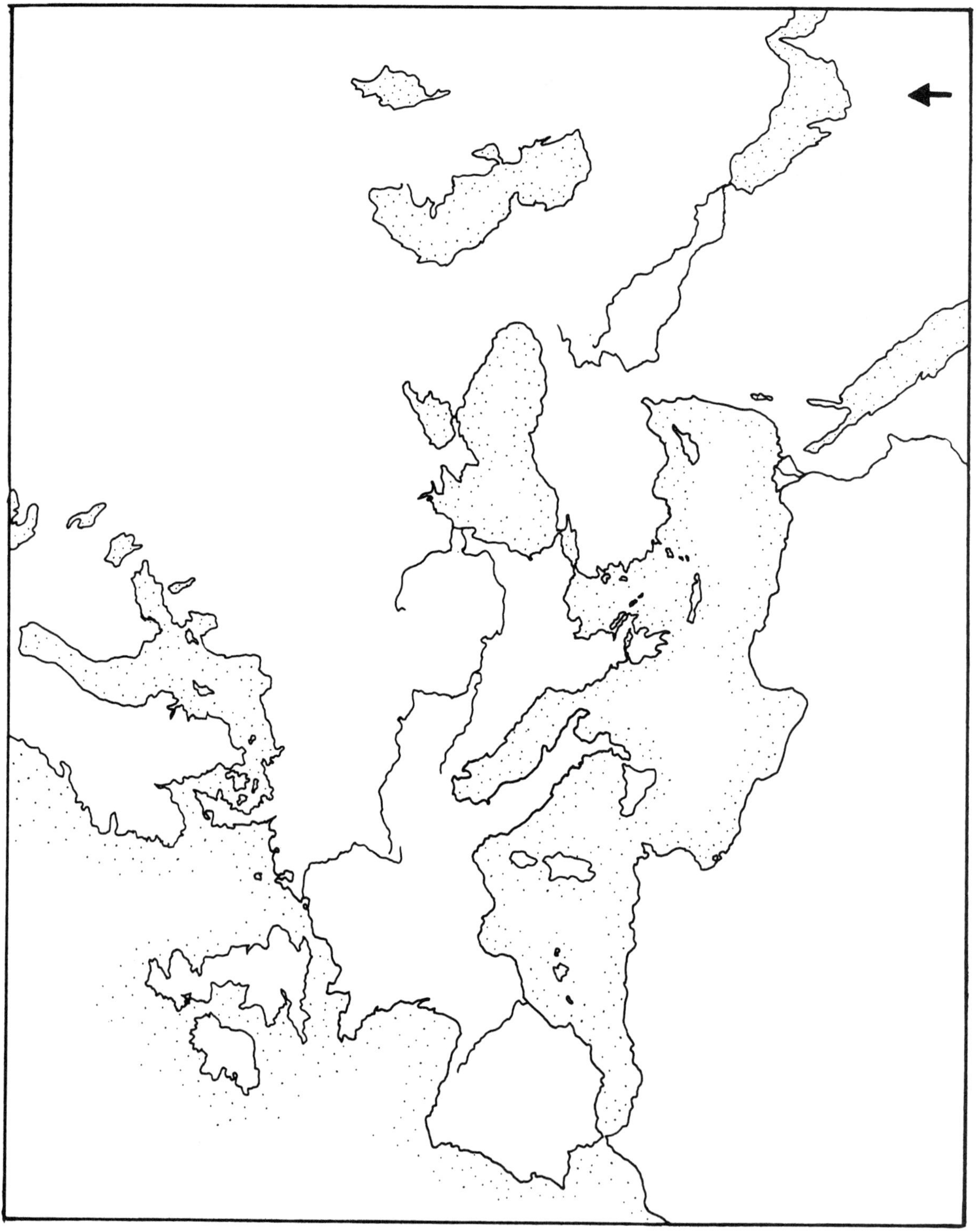

Exercise 15
Revolution and Unification: Europe in 1871

Introduction

Despite the attempts to keep the lid on change, a new wave of revolution and reform spread across Europe in the second half of the nineteenth century. Again the French took a leading role. The 1830's to the 1850's saw revolts in Spain, Portugal, France, Italy, Russia and Poland. By the 1870's the map of Europe had again changed.

Locations

On the map provided draw the boundaries of and number the following European states and regions as of 1871.

A. States:

1. Austria-Hungary
2. Belgium
3. Denmark
4. France
5. German Empire
6. Great Britain
7. Greece
8. Italy
9. Ottoman Empire
10. Spain
11. Switzerland

B. Regions:

12. Albania
13. Bosnia
14. Croatia-Slovenia
15. Serbia

Questions

Briefly explain the process by which Italy and Germany became unified. What main factors allowed them to unify?

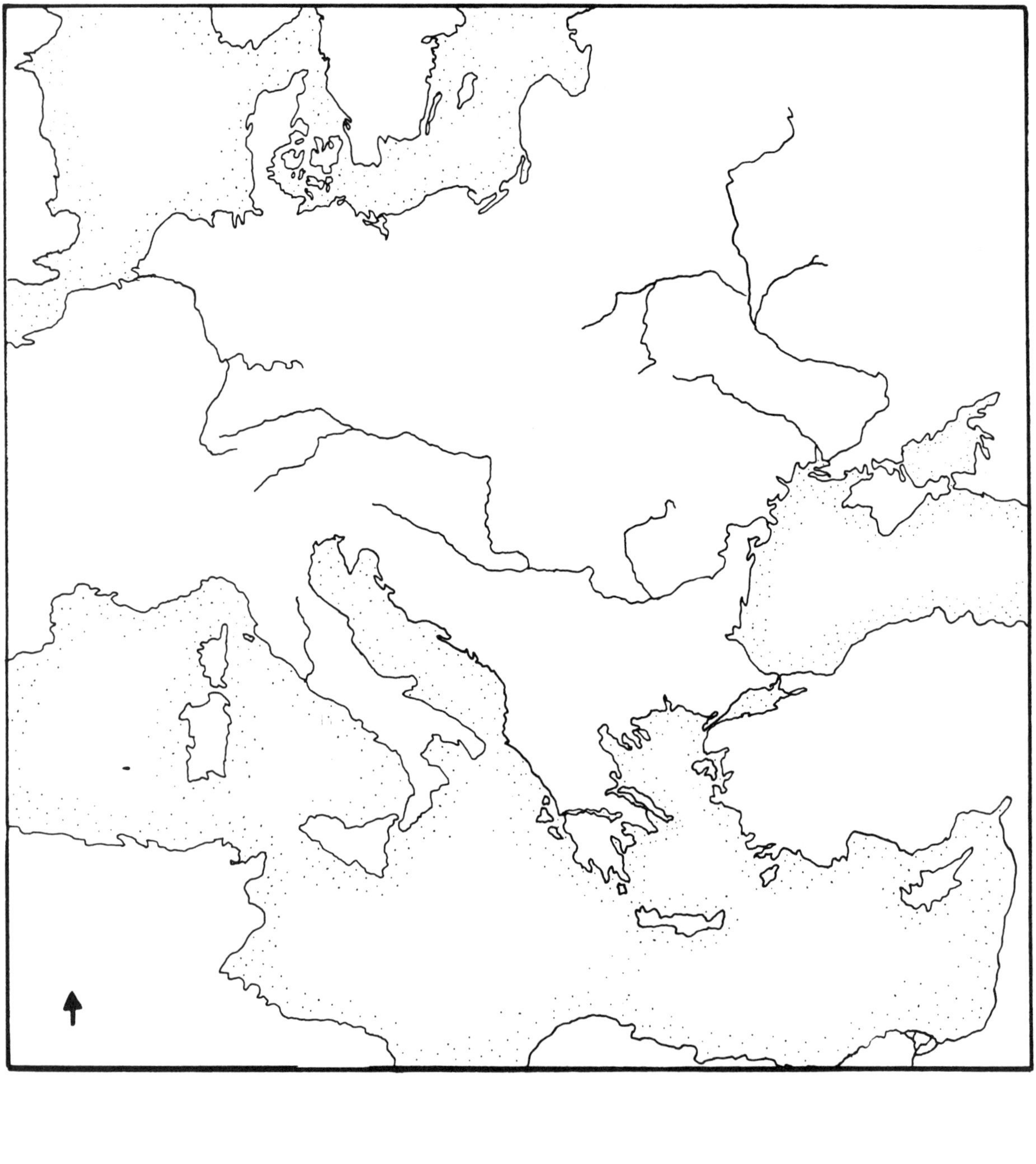

Exercise 16
The Balkans: 1878-1913

Introduction

Crises in the Balkans have commonly occurred over the centuries. In 1908 the Balkan states of Bosnia and Herzegovina were annexed by Austria. The Serbs, because their hopes for a larger Serbian kingdom were dashed, responded by precipitating an international incident. In 1912 more attention was drawn to the region when the Ottoman Turks were defeated in the First Balkan war. New divisions of territories resulted. 1913 saw another war and further divisions of the Balkans. This exercise traces these divisions of the Balkans prior to World War I.

Locations

With different colored pencils outline the boundaries of the Balkan states after 1871. Next in different colors, trace the boundaries of and number the Balkan states as of 1913.

A. Balkan states after the Congress of Berlin in 1878

1. Albania
2. Bulgaria
3. Croatia
4. Greece
5. Hungary
6. Macedonia
7. Serbia
8. Slovenia

B. Balkan states as of 1913.

8. Albania
9. Austria-Hungary
10. Bulgaria
11. Greece
12. Montenegro
13. Rumania
14. Serbia

Questions

What happened to Macedonia? What happened to the Ottoman possessions in the Balkans? And under whose control were the Bosnians and Herzegovinians?

What were the goals and motivations of the Serbians in the Balkan wars? Were they successful in reaching their goals? What were the long-term results of the Balkan Wars?

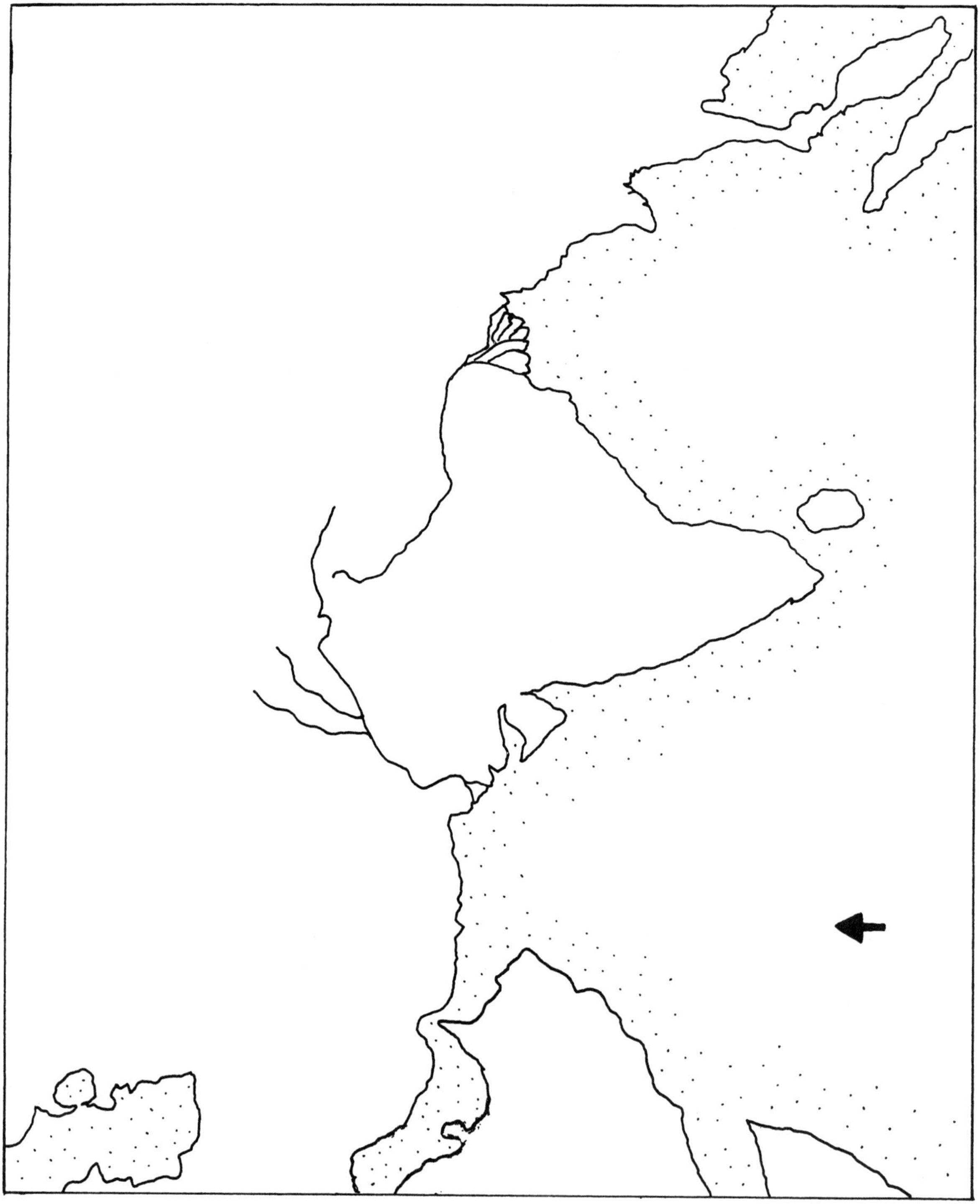

Exercise 17
India: 17th - 20th Centuries

Introduction

India, like other most other Asian countries, was exploited by western powers for centuries. Restrictive colonial policies would eventually give rise to strong nationalistic movements, which were able to overthrow the foreign colonial powers. For example in a dramatic movement, led by Gandhi, the British were expelled from India in the 20th century. This exercise looks at the regions, cities and environment of India.

Locations

On the map provided shade in and number the following geographical features, regions and cities.

A. Geographical features

1. Arabian Sea
2. Bay of Bengal
3. Ganges River
4. Indian Ocean
5. Indus River

B. Regions

6. Assam
7. Bengal
8. Burma
9. Ceylon
10. Kashmir
11. Marathas
12. Mysor
13. Punjab

C. Cities

14. Bangalore
15. Benares
16. Bhopal
17. Bombay
18. Calcutta
19. Delhi
20. Hyderabad
21. Lahore
22. Simla

D. Boundaries

23. Bangladesh (20th century)
24. India under British control in the 19th century
25. Pakistan (20th century)

Questions

How did India win its independence form the British? Why did it then split into several independent nations? Explain why, and over what areas, China and India still have boundary disputes.

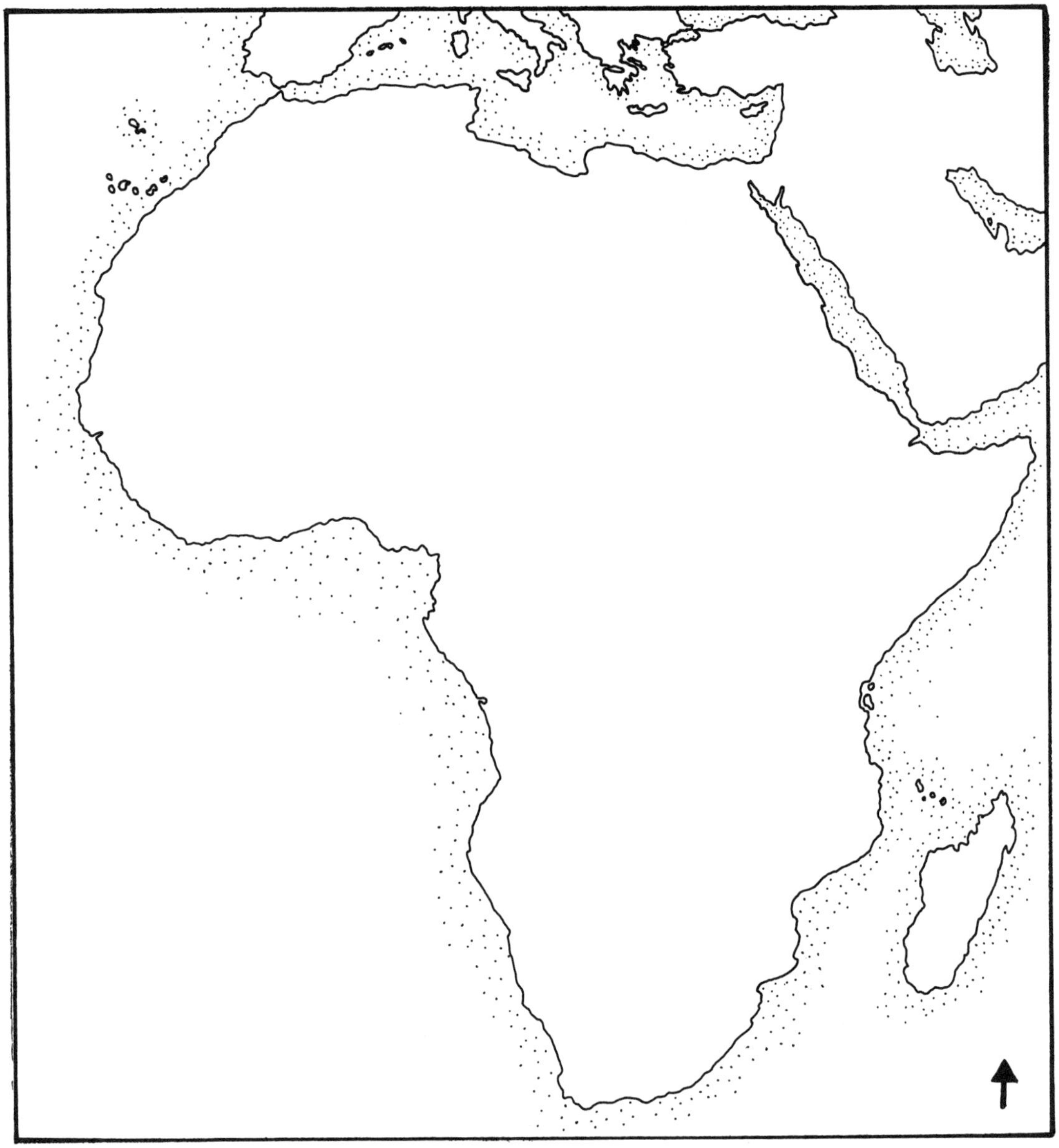

Exercise 18

Africa: European Control in 1914

Introduction

In the latter years of the nineteenth century European states were again interested in overseas expansion. The Americas were lost to them so they renewed their attentions toward Asia and Africa. They were not, however, able to dominate the territories in Asia and Africa quite like they had done in earlier centuries. Still, these new colonies were worth the trouble as they provided many benefits, both material and social.

Locations

Africa was carved up among the Europeans, with only Ethiopia and Liberia as independent nations. With different colored pencils, color in and identify (for example, make all French territory blue) the territory claimed by the following colonial powers. Also mark the boundaries of the following states and regions.

A. Colonial powers

1. Belgium
2. Boer Republic
3. France
4. Germany
5. Great Britain
6. Italy
7. Portugal

B. States and regions

8. Algeria
9. Angola
10. Congo
11. Ethiopia
12. Kenya
13. Liberia
14. Madagascar
15. South Africa

Questions

What were the benefits (economic, social, political) of African colonies to the Europeans? Briefly, what were some of the effects of this colonialism on the continent of Africa? Why were Liberia and Ethiopia able to remain independent?

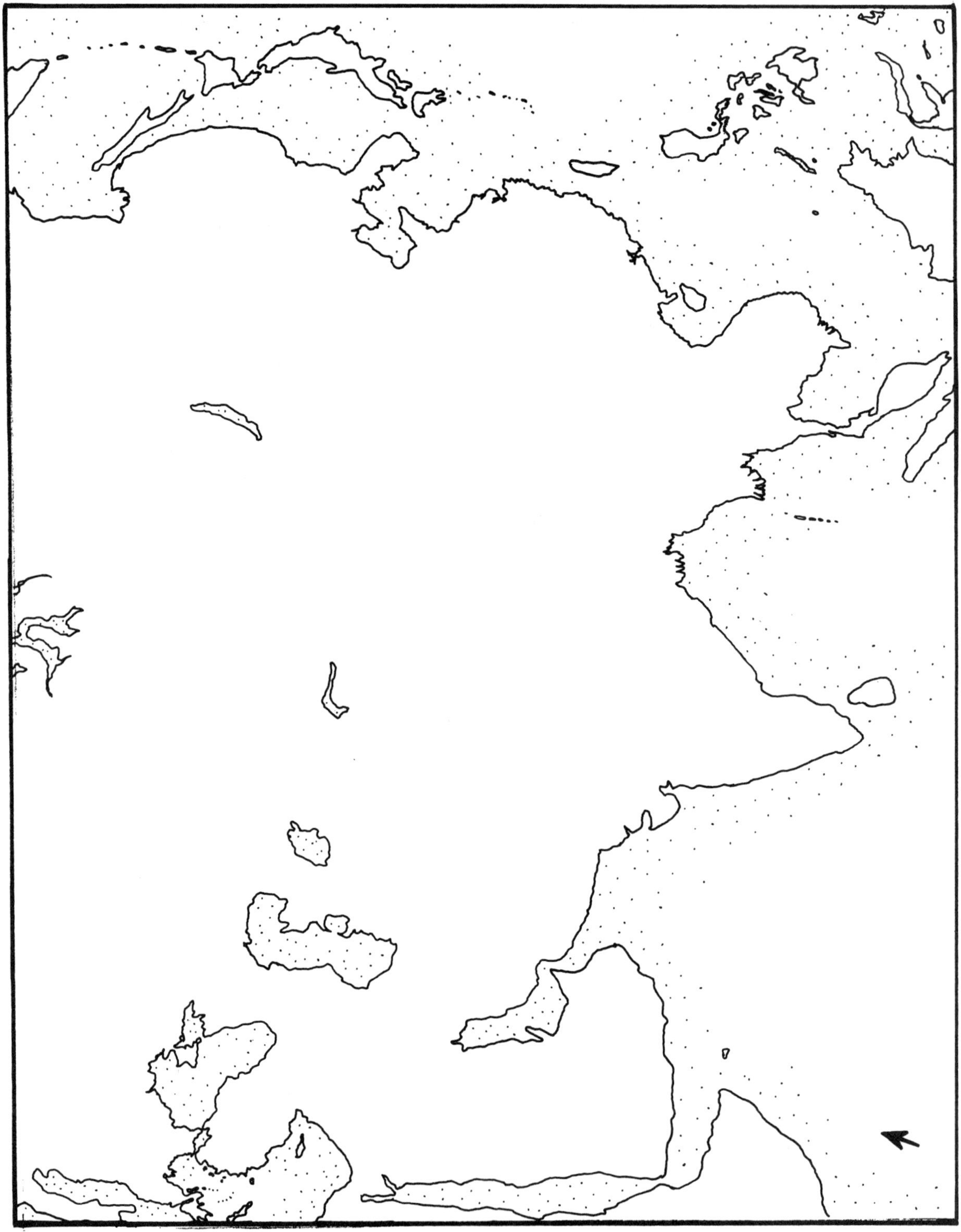

Exercise 19

Asia: European Influences in 1914

Introduction

Asia, too, received the attentions of the Europeans. Some territories were acquired by the Europeans, others came strongly under the influence of the western powers. The United States also evinced an interest in the Pacific rim countries and claimed some territory for themselves. These western states felt themselves superior to the Asian and African people, and thus easily justified their imperialistic attitude by explaining that such oppression was of mutual benefit. Kipling's poem the "White Man's Burden" exemplifies this western feeling of superiority.

Locations

On the map provided identify the areas of western possessions and spheres of influence, Next place the number of the following regions on your map.

A. Possessions/spheres of influence

1. Dutch
2. Germany
3. Great Britain
4. Portugal
5. Russia
6. United States

B. Regions

7. Ceylon
8. China
9. East Indies
10. India
11. Japan
12. Korea
13. Persia
14. Philippines
15. Tibet

Questions

Compare and contrast British and Russian interests in Asia. What attracted each to the region? How did the Russians and British interact? With what results for the people of Asia? Which territories remained independent? How did they manage to remain so?

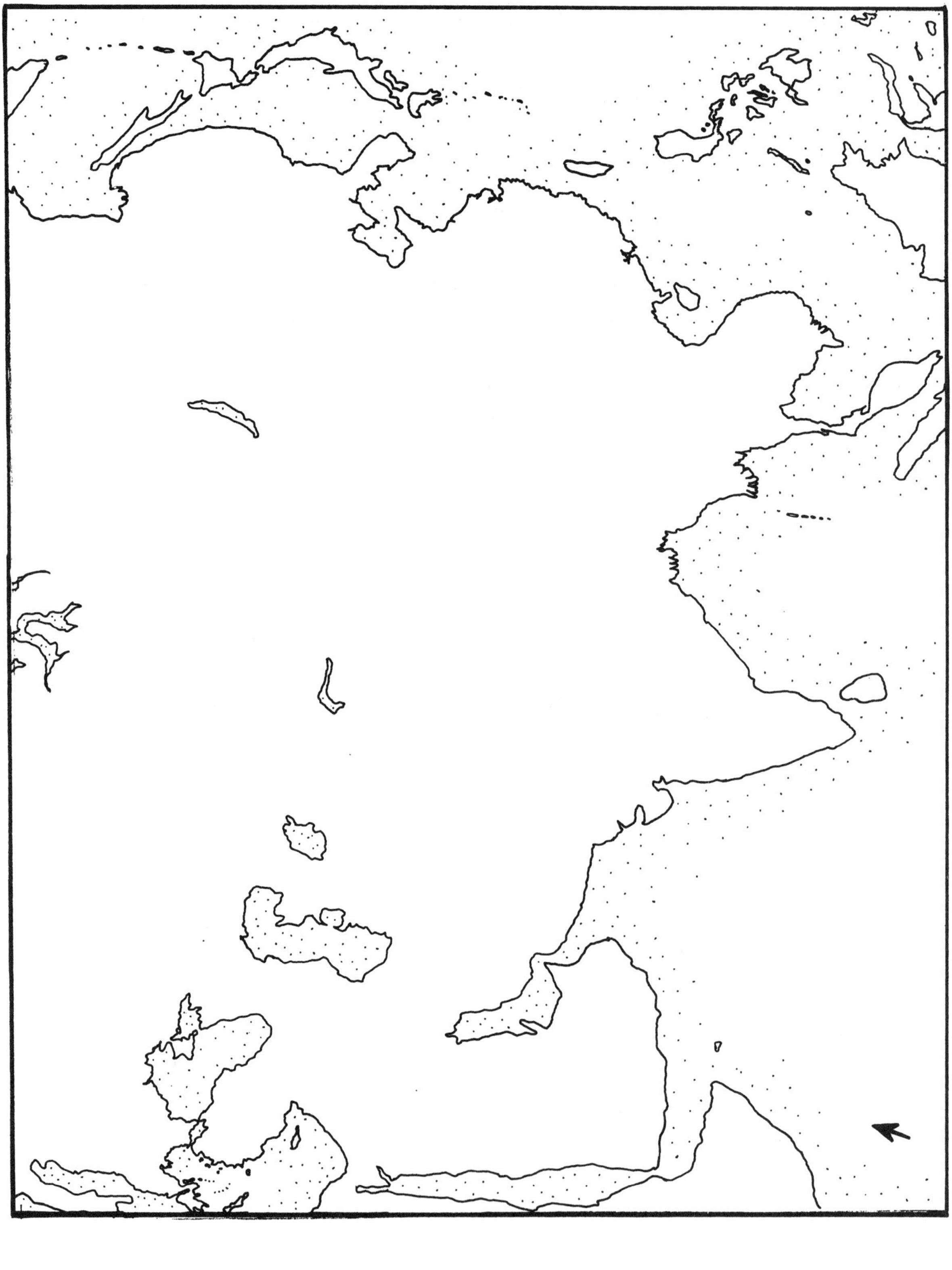

Exercise 20
China and Japan into the 20th Century

Introduction

In about 1868 Japan's interest in the outside world increased dramatically. By 1875 Japan had gained control of several islands. Japan continued to extend her empire to the north, the south and to the mainland by means of a series of three wars.

In China, the 20th century has seen profound changes. Participation in the Long March defined a generation of Chinese. The Chinese today are the most populous nation on earth and the greatest communist power in the 1990's. This exercise traces the spheres of influence exerted over time by both the Chinese and Japanese.

Locations

With different colored pencils, lightly shade in and number the following areas of foreign influence, locate the following regions, cities and geographical features and trace the boundaries of the Chinese state at 1911 and 1950.

A. Areas of influences

1. British
2. Japanese in 1918
3. Russian

B. Regions and cities

4. Amoy
5. Beijing
6. Canton
7. Hong Kong
8. Hunan
9. Macao
10. Manchuria
11. Philippines
12. Quingdao
13. Russia
14. Taipei
15. Taiwan
16. Vladivostok
17. Xinjing

C. Geographical features

18. Altai Mountains
19. Pacific Ocean
20. Sea of Japan
21. South China Sea

D. Boundaries

22. Chinese Empire as of 1911
23. Chinese State as of ca. 1950
24. Japanese possessions 1875
25. Japanese acquisitions 1894-1914

Questions

List the areas acquired by Japan as of 1875 and as of 1914. What conflicts, if any, resulted from these acquisitions? What were the long term effects of these acquisitions?

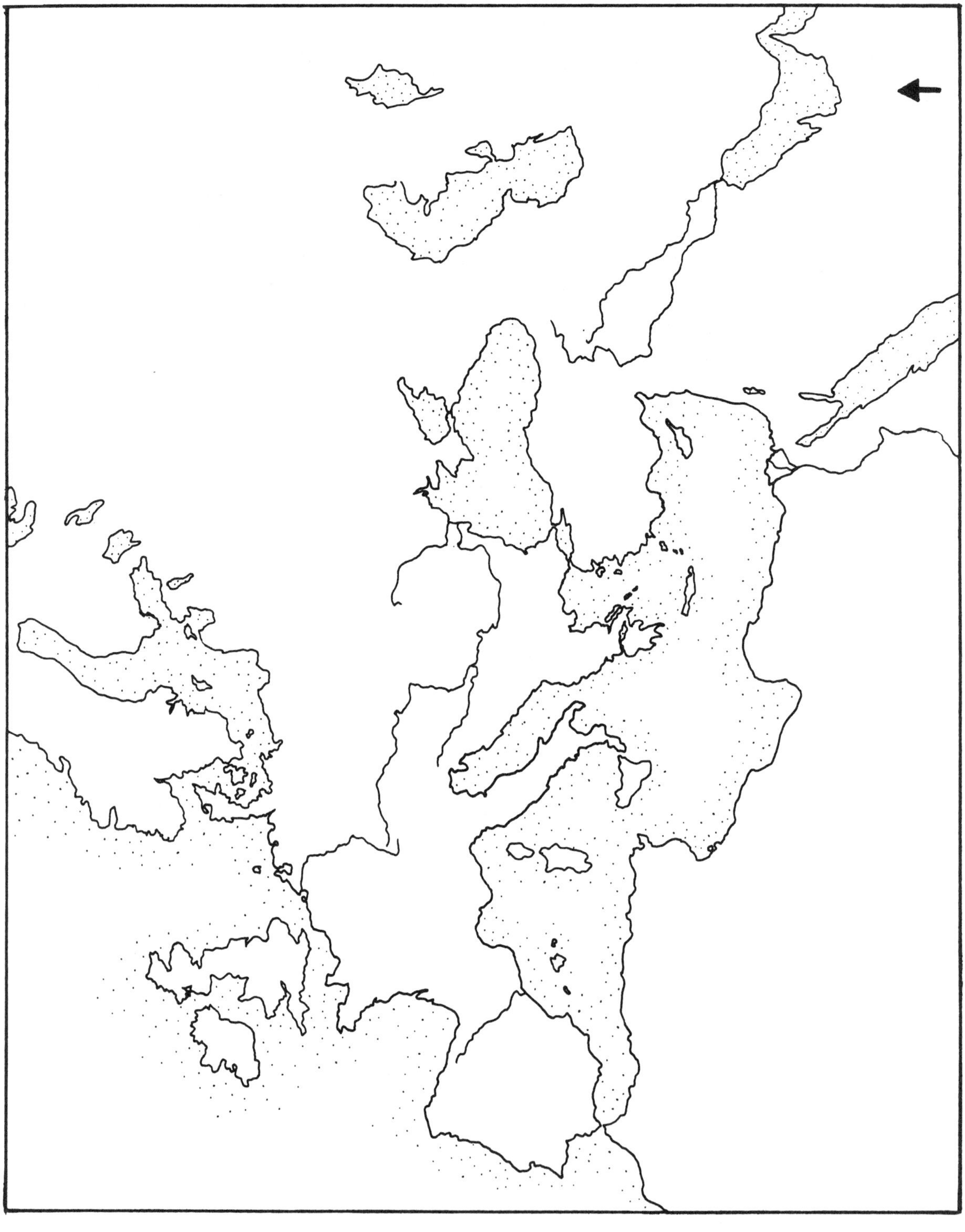

Exercise 21

Europe after World War I

Introduction

World War I was one of the defining events of the twentieth century. The brutality, overwhelming magnitude, the length of the war, and its final settlement would prepare the road for yet another major conflict. Its destructiveness was a shock and disappointment to Europeans -- intellectual, industrial worker and farmer alike. Not surprisingly, the conflict was ignited by a confrontation between Austria and Serbia, after the heir to the Austrian throne was assassinated in Sarajevo, a Bosnian city.

This exercise compares the political divisions of Europe before and after the "Great War."

Locations

The boundary lines in this exercise will be complicated, so please draw neatly and carefully. On the map provided use a single colored, dotted, line to mark the boundaries of pre-World War I Europe, then clearly number these states. Next, with a single colored solid line, trace the post World War I boundaries and number the second set of states.

A. Pre W.W.I boundaries

1. Albania
2. Austria-Hungary
3. Belgium
4. Bulgaria
5. France
6. Germany
7. Greece
8. Italy
9. Montenegro
10. Netherlands
11. Rumania
12. Russia
13. Serbia
14. Spain
15. Switzerland

B. Post World War I boundaries

16. Albania
17. Austria
18. Bulgaria
19. Czechoslovakia
20. France
21. Germany
22. Hungary
23. Poland
24. Rumania
25. Yugoslavia

Questions

Where did Yugoslavia and Czechoslovakia come from? What happened to the territory of the Germans after the war? Who gained by Germany's losses? How did the Austro-Hungarian Empire fare in the new divisions of Europe? Finally, what result did this war have on European dominance of world affairs?

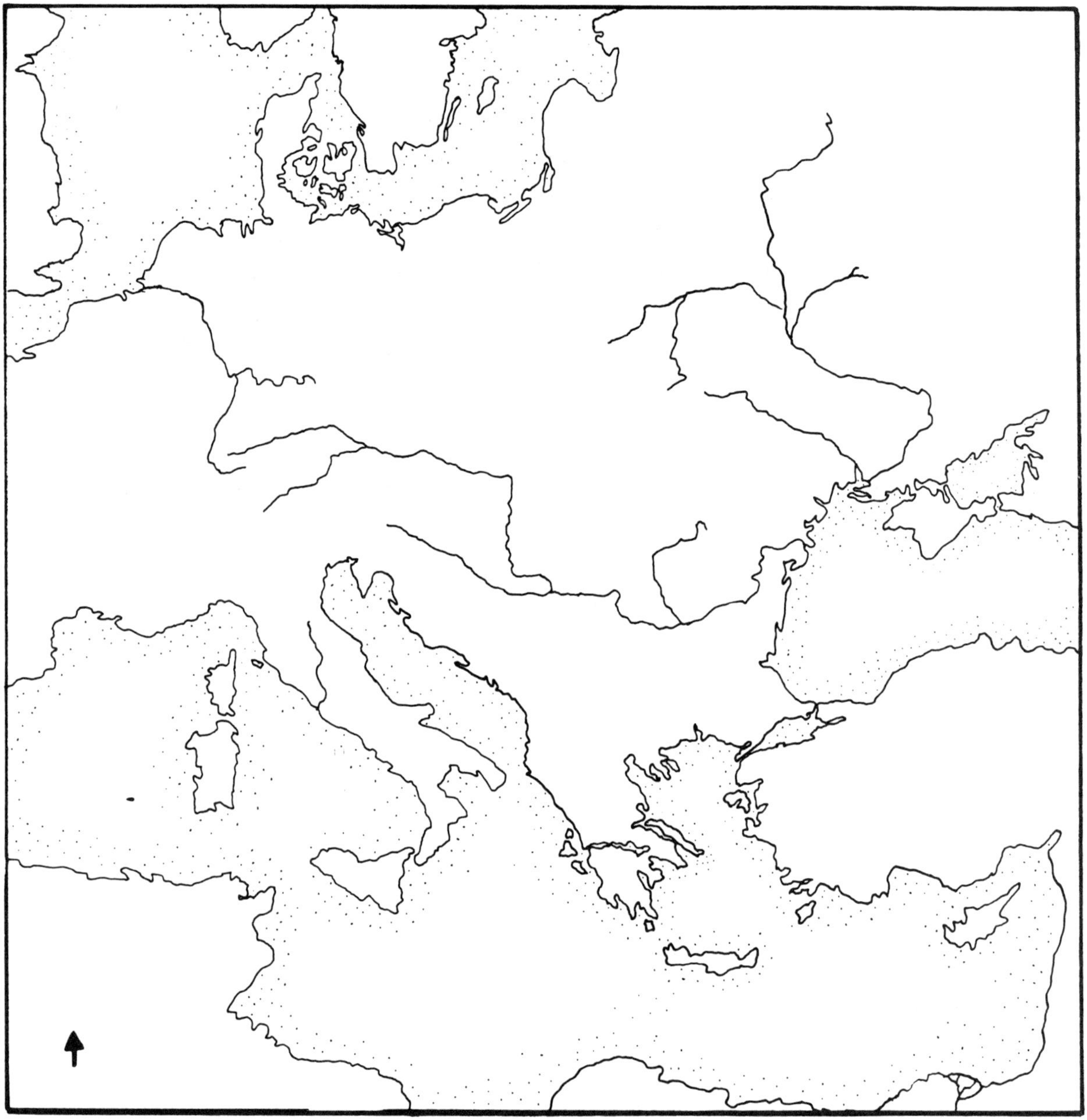

Exercise 22
Central Europe after World War II

Introduction

In 1919 the people of Europe were optimistic, but soon the Great Depression hit, affecting Americans and Europeans alike. The Germans suffered severely from these financial setbacks and came to resent their position in the post war world. According to Heinrich Hauser "An almost unbroken chain of homeless men extends the whole length of the great Hamburg-Berlin highway..." This economic disaster precipitated non-democratic political solutions to economic problems and led to the creation of authoritarian and totalitarian states. World War II began after the Nazi's took power in Germany and convinced the German people that, among other things, they needed and deserved more living space (*lebensraum*). Another massively destructive war was fought, with devastating demographic, material and psychological results. Here we will look at one result: the territorial settlement of Central Europe following the war.

Locations

Number and draw in the 1949 boundaries, then using different colored pencils shade in and number the US, French, British and Soviet zones in Germany. Trace the boundaries of the territory gained by the Soviet Union and mark with a dotted line the "Iron Curtain" (erected 1955)and place the following geographical features on your map.

A. Boundaries at 1949

1. Czechoslovakia
2. Estonia
3. Finland
4. France
5. Germany
6. Greece
7. Hungary
8. Latvia
9. Lithuania
10. Poland
11. Yugoslavia

B. Allied Zones

12. British
13. French
14. Soviet
15. US

C. Boundaries of the Soviet Union

16. "Iron Curtain"
17. Land gained by the USSR

D. Geographical features:

18. Danube River
19. Oder River
20. Rhine River

Questions

What were the general affects of this war on the population of Europe? How long was Germany divided into Zones? What territory was lost to Germany and to whom did it go? Territorially, who gained the most from the settlement after World War II?

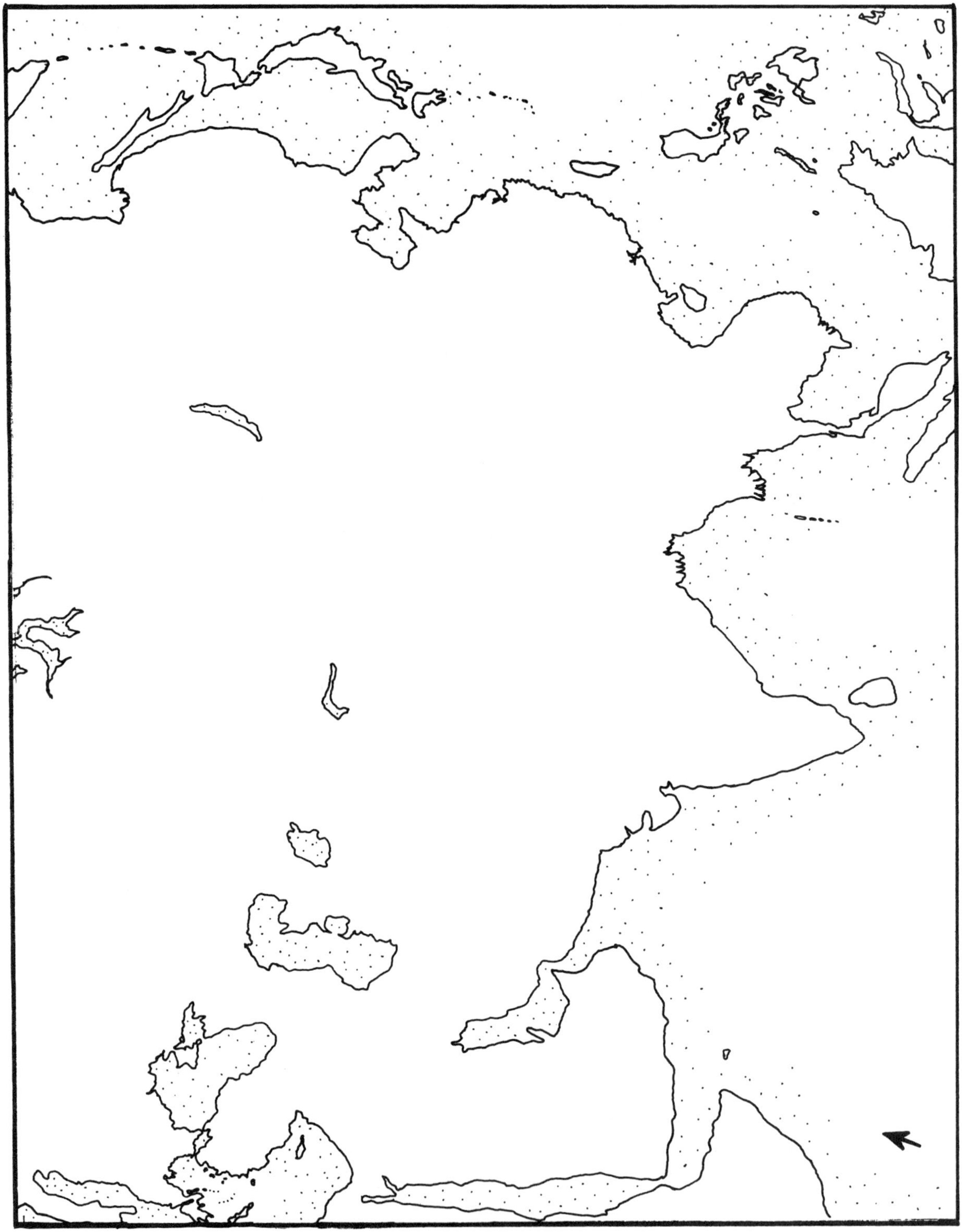

Exercise 23
The Soviet Union

Introduction

The communist revolution in Russia eventually led to the development of one of the twentieth centuries superpowers: the Soviet Union. The dream was of a socialist state of unprecedented fairness and justice. Yet the Soviet Union held fast to territories in Eastern Europe and Asia in a fashion that belied its utopian rhetoric.

This exercise introduces you to the territories under the control of the, now former, Soviet Union.

Locations

Clearly mark then number the boundaries of the following states and regions and then add the following cities and geographical features.

A. States and regions

1. Belarus
2. Estonia
3. Kazakhistan
4. Lithuania
5. Moldavia
6. Poland
7. Romania
8. Ukraine

B. Cities

9. Bucharest
10. Helsinki
11. Kiev
12. Minsk
13. Moscow
14. Warsaw

C. Geographical features

15. Baltic Sea
16. Black Sea
17. Caspian Sea
18. Danube River
19. Dneiper River
20. Volga River

Questions

What role did Stalin play in the development of the cold war? What were contemporary Soviet attitudes towards Stalin and how did these affect policies (if at all)? What were the main factors that caused the end of the cold war and the collapse of the USSR? What role did Gorbachev play in this political transformation?

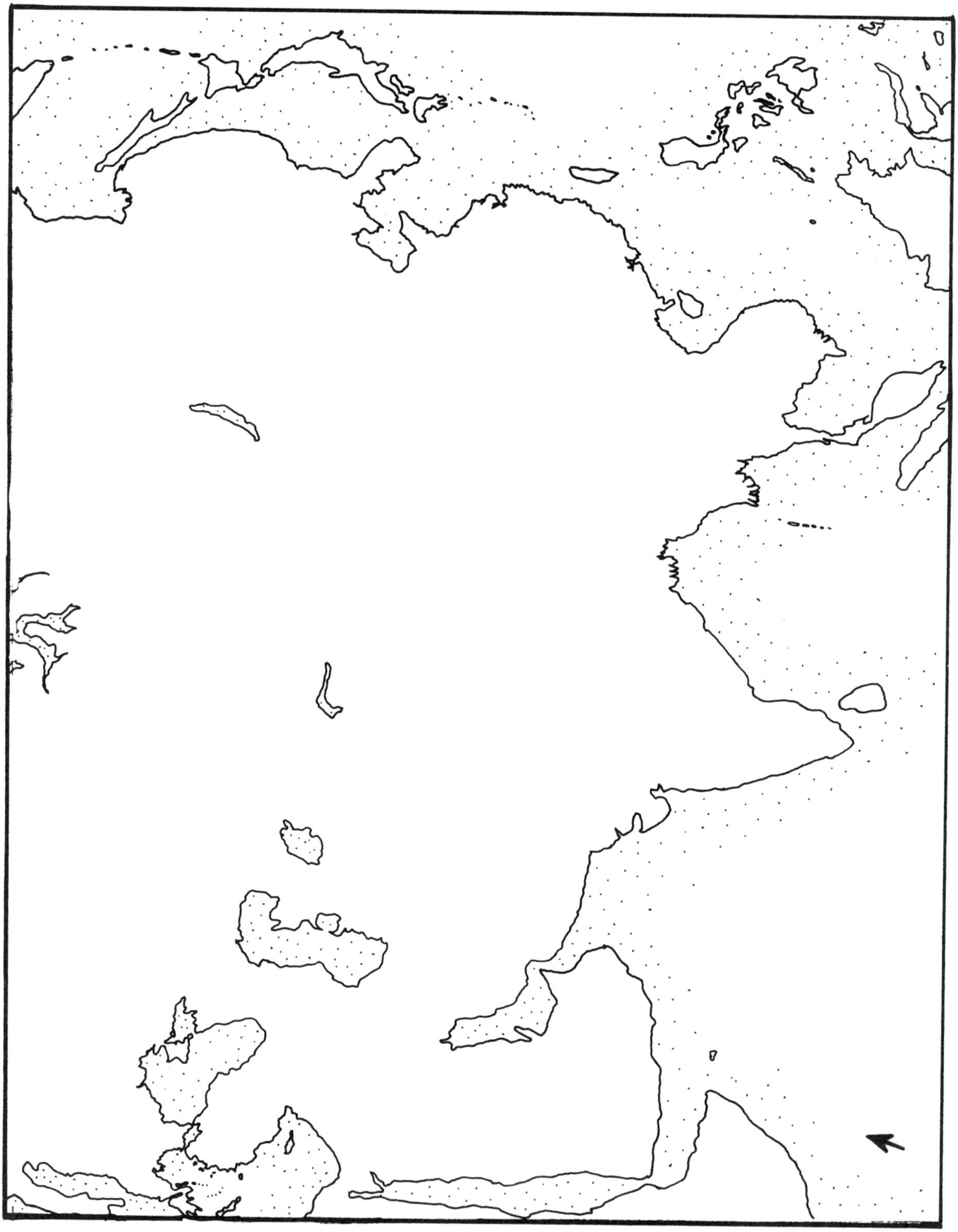

Exercise 24

The Far East and Asia in the Later 20th Century

Introduction

Our world of the 20th century continues to transform itself. This exercise introduces you to the countries of Asia after World War II, revolutions, the Korean and Vietnam conflicts. These conflicts spurred the creation of new boundaries -- boundaries that are no more set in stone now than they had been in the centuries preceding ours.

Locations

On the map provided draw the boundaries and number the following states of the Far East and locate and number the following major cities.

A. States

1. Bangladesh
2. Cambodia
3. India
4. Japan
5. Laos
6. Mongolia
7. North Korea
8. Pakistan
9. Philippines
10. Russia
11. South Korea
12. Taiwan (Republic of China)
13. Thailand
14. The People's Republic of China
15. Tibet
16. Vietnam

B. Cities

17. Bangkok
18. Bombay
19. Hiroshima
20. Hong Kong
21. Kwangju
22. Kyoto
23. Lhasa
24. Manila
25. Nagasaki
26. New Delhi
27. Rangoon
28. Shanghai
29. Seoul
30. Tokyo

Questions

How has communism helped shape the states of Asia? What factors in the cultures of the Asian people contributed to their attraction to communism? What problems did the communist system solve? In what ways has it been successful in its goals? Unsuccessful?

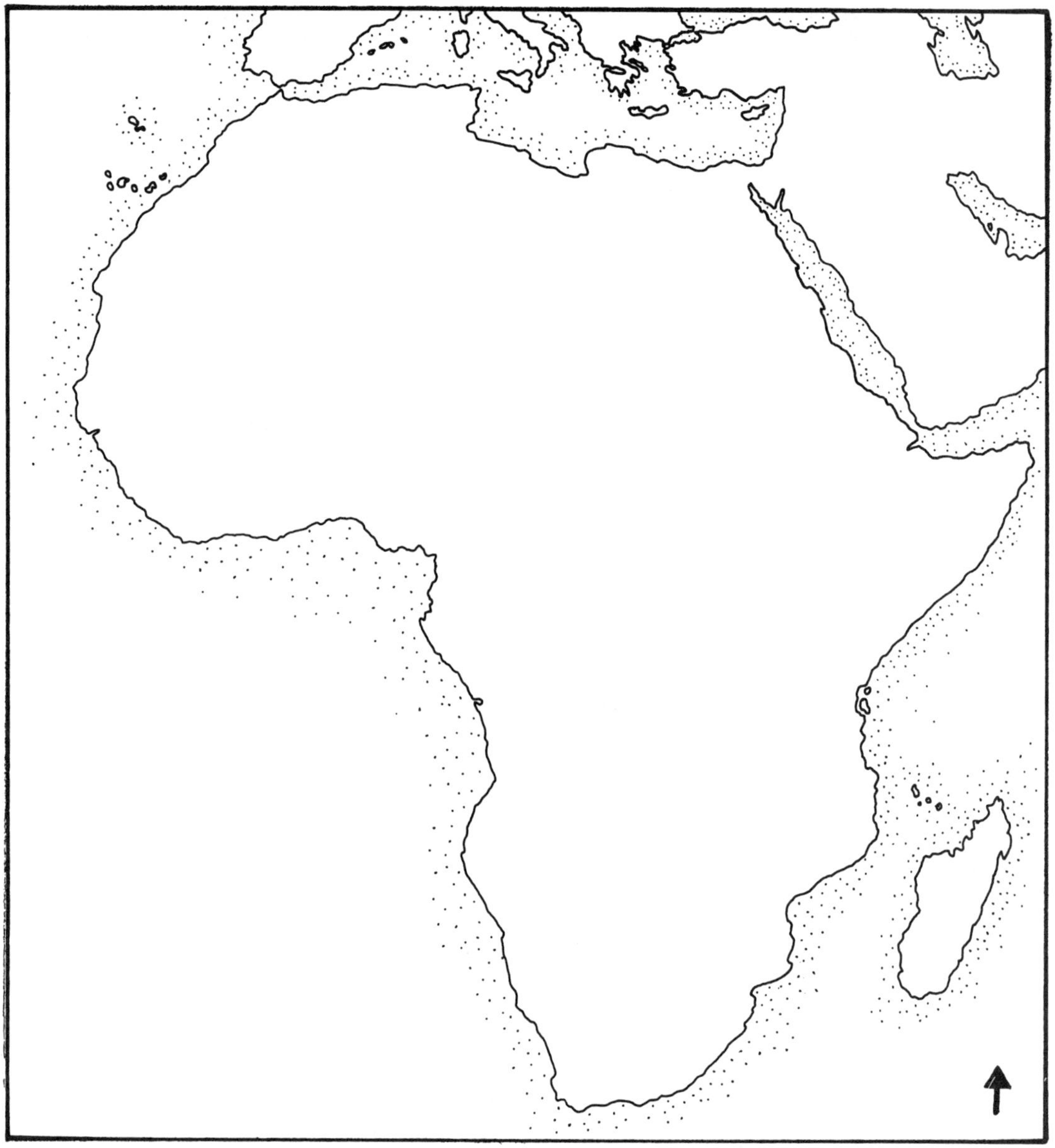

Exercise 25
Africa, the Near East and the Mediterranean after World War II

Introduction

Like other regions of the world, the countries of Africa and the Near East have spent the better part of the 20th century freeing themselves from the colonial and imperial powers. The boundaries of the African countries reflect colonial territories rather than "natural" cultural or economic regions. This fact has increased conflict and hindered the ability of some African states to rule and support themselves successfully and peacefully.

The states of the Arabian peninsula have proved more fortunate economically, due to their abundant and necessary resources (oil). This exercise introduces you to modern Africa and the Near East.

Locations

Draw in the boundaries, number the states, and locate the following geographical features for the regions of Africa and Arabia.

A. Africa
1. Algeria
2. Angola
3. Egypt
4. Ethiopia
5. Ghana
6. Ivory Coast
7. Liberia
8. Libya
9. Morocco
10. Mozambique
11. Namibia
12. Nigeria
13. Republic of South Africa
14. Sudan
15. Tanzania

B. Arabia
16. Bahrain
17. Jordan
18. Kuwait
19. Saudi Arabia
20. South Yemen
21. Yemen

C. Geographical features
22. Cyprus
23. Greece
24. Iraq
25. Israel
26. Italy
27. Mediterranean Sea
28. Persian Gulf
29. Red Sea
30. Turkey

Questions

What are the economic problems facing many of the Saharan and sub-Saharan African countries? What are the differences in the resources found in the east, west and southern tip of Africa? What have been the long term results of this uneven distribution of natural resources?

Exercise 26
The Middle East and Asia After World War II

Introduction

World War II had a profound impact in the territories influenced and claimed by the European powers in Africa, Asia and the Middle East. Claims of independence and nationalistic anti-colony movements abounded. In Asia and the Middle East successful revolutionary attempts added up. India and Pakistan freed themselves from British rule. Other Asian countries also managed to loose the bonds of European control. In the Middle East, the growing nationalism of the Arabs helped put an end to colonial control, but they could not prevent the creation of a new Jewish state, Israel.

Locations

On the map provided draw the boundaries, number and where appropriate provide the date of independence for the following states of the Middle East and Asia.

1. Bangladesh
2. Burma
3. Cambodia
4. India
5. Israel
6. Jordan
7. Kuwait
8. Laos
9. Lebanon
10. Pakistan
11. Philippines
12. Saudi Arabia
13. Syria
14. Turkey
15. Vietnam

Questions

At the end of World War II a new conflict arose between the two major "super-powers," the erstwhile allies, the United States and Soviet Union. Briefly describe the nature of this conflict prior to 1980. What effect did their relations have on the politics of the Middle East? What specific factors generally encouraged the collapse of the European colonies?

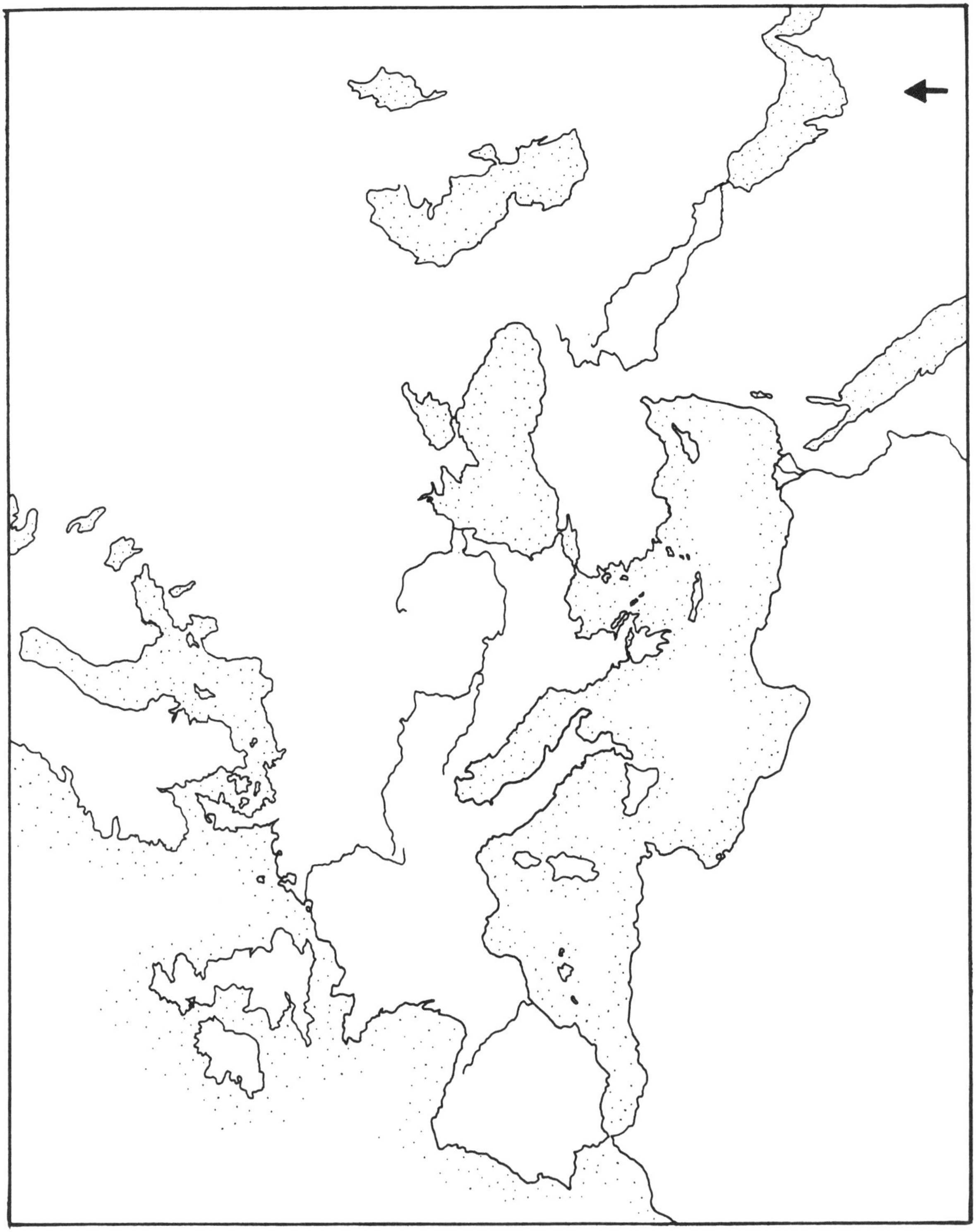

Exercise 27

The Future: Political and Cultural Boundaries in Europe

Introduction

You have seen the boundaries of the European world change continually over time. This is an exercise of your imagination. On the map provided draw the boundaries of Europe as you believe they will be fifty years from today. Mark on your map major changes in population that you predict (do you think large numbers, for example, of ethnic Albanians will move to another country or countries?). Do you believe there will be any more major wars on the order of the first and second world wars? Why or why not?

Next justify your predictions. Why do you believe the changes you suggest will occur? Use both current and past events to support your position.

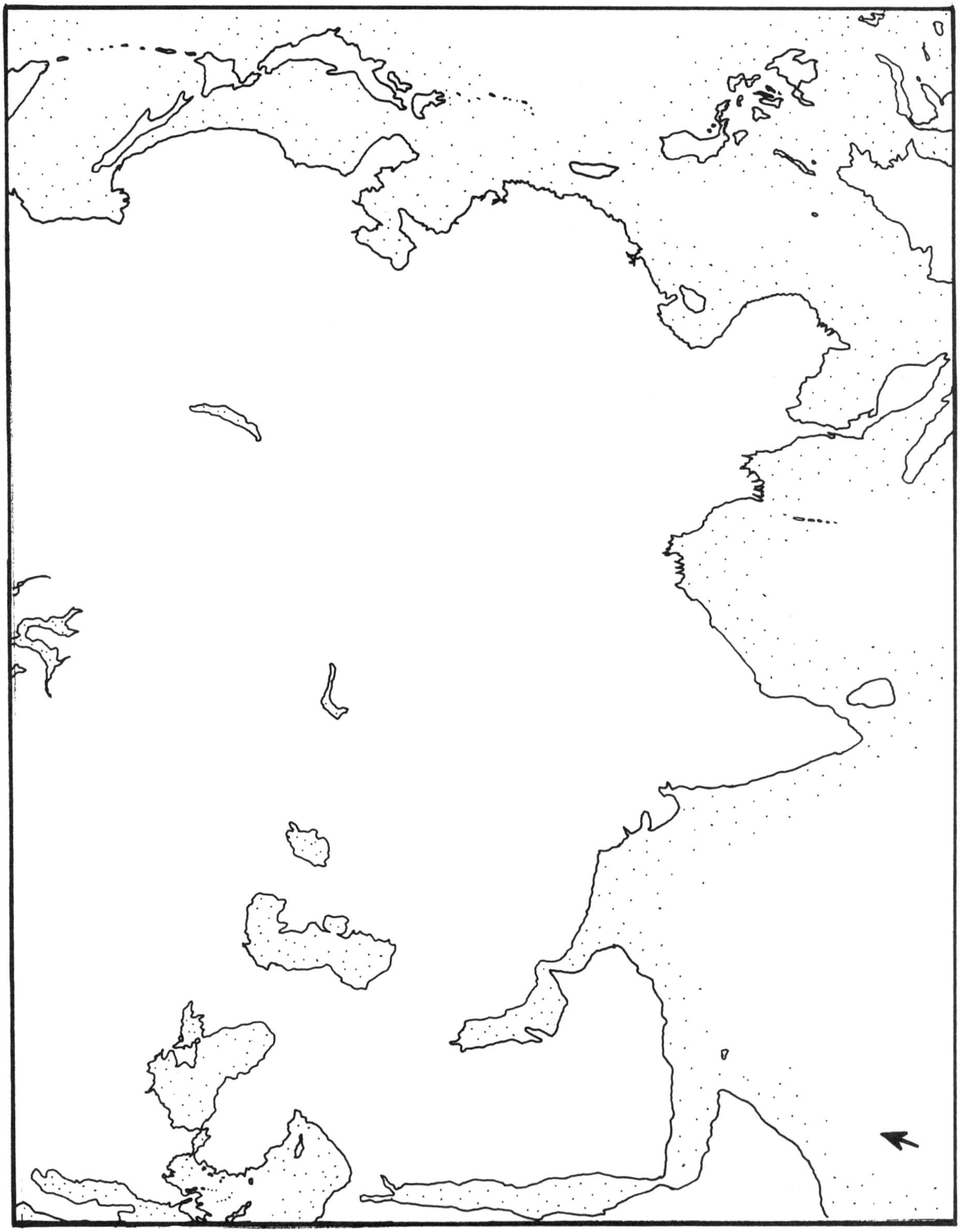

Exercise 28

The Future: Political and Cultural Boundaries in Asia

Introduction

You have also seen the boundaries of the Asian world change continually over time. This is an exercise of your imagination. On the map provided draw the boundaries of Asia as you believe they will be fifty years from today. Mark on your map major changes in population that you predict. (Do you think, for example, that population control measures in India will be successful?) Do you believe there will be any more major wars on the order of the first and second world wars? Why or why not?

Next justify your predictions. Why do you believe the changes you suggest will occur? Use both current and past events to support your position.

Extra Maps

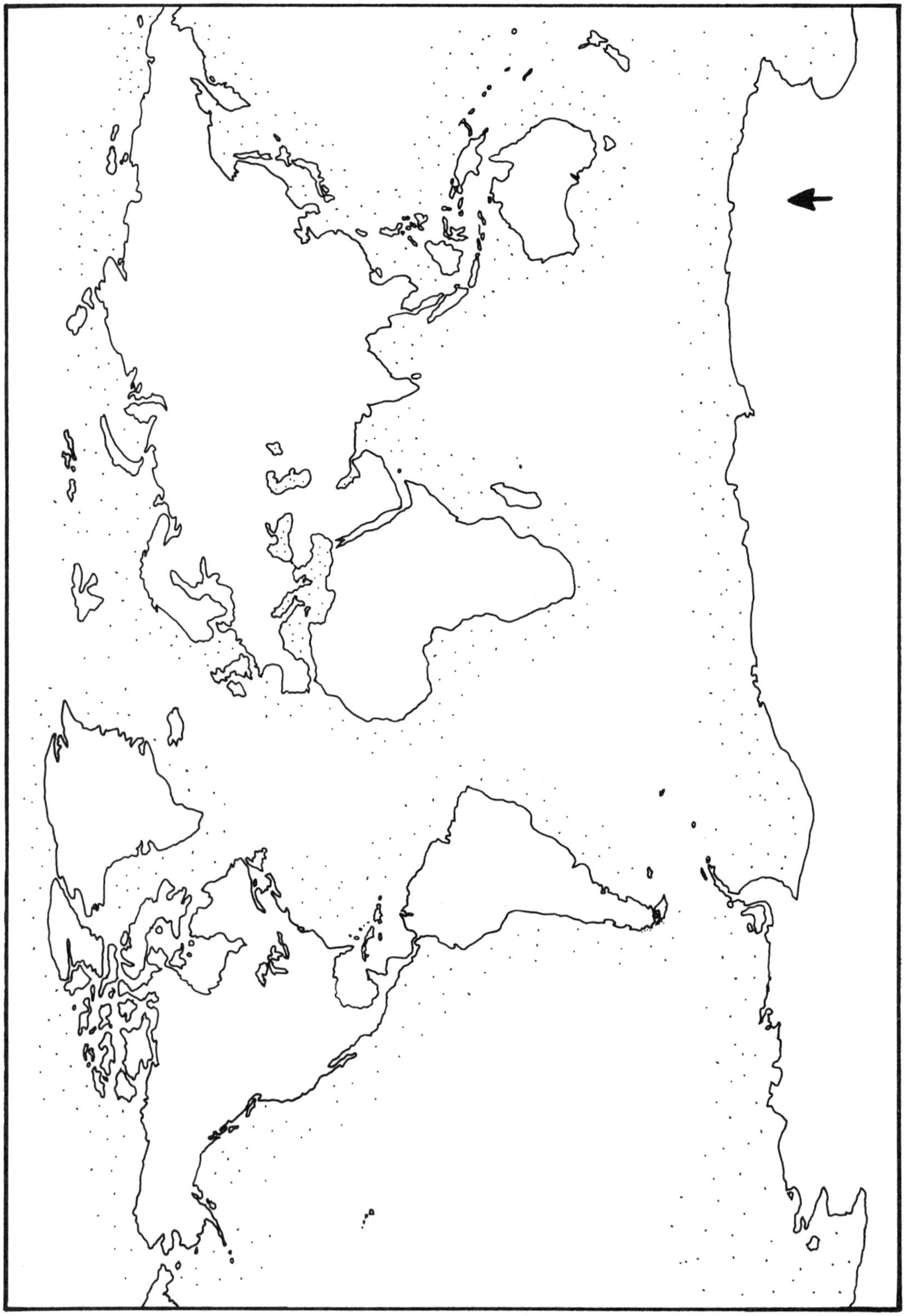

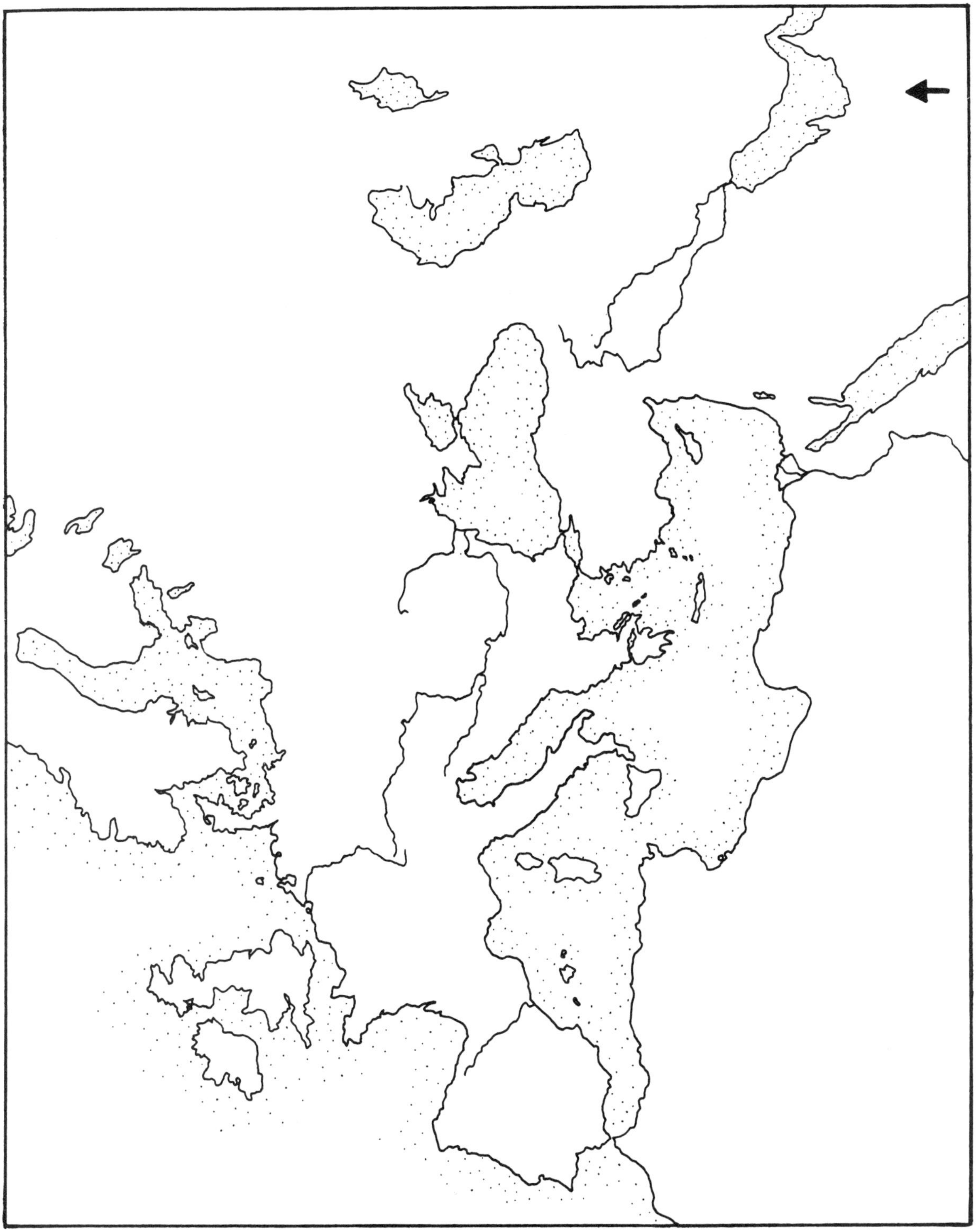

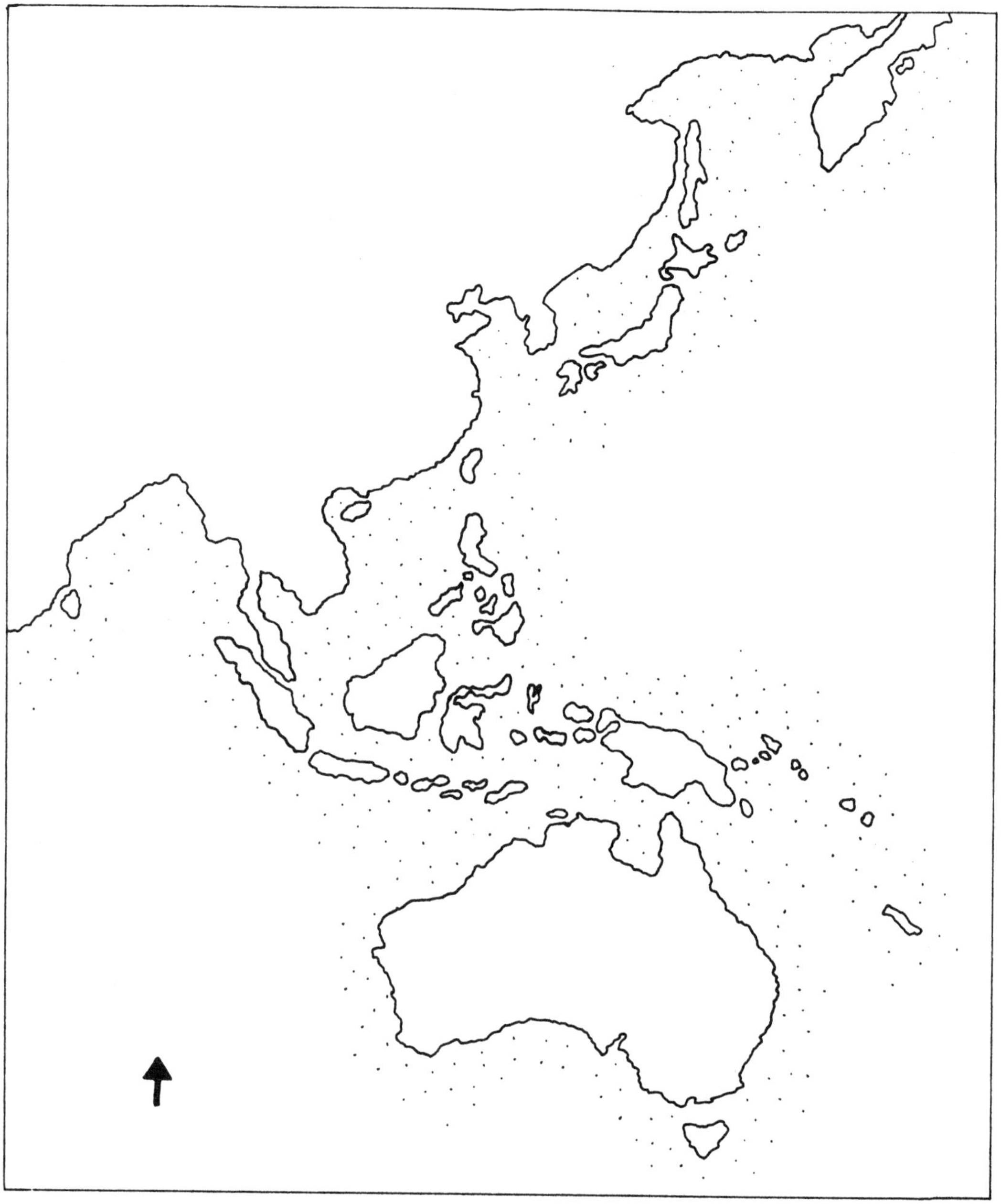

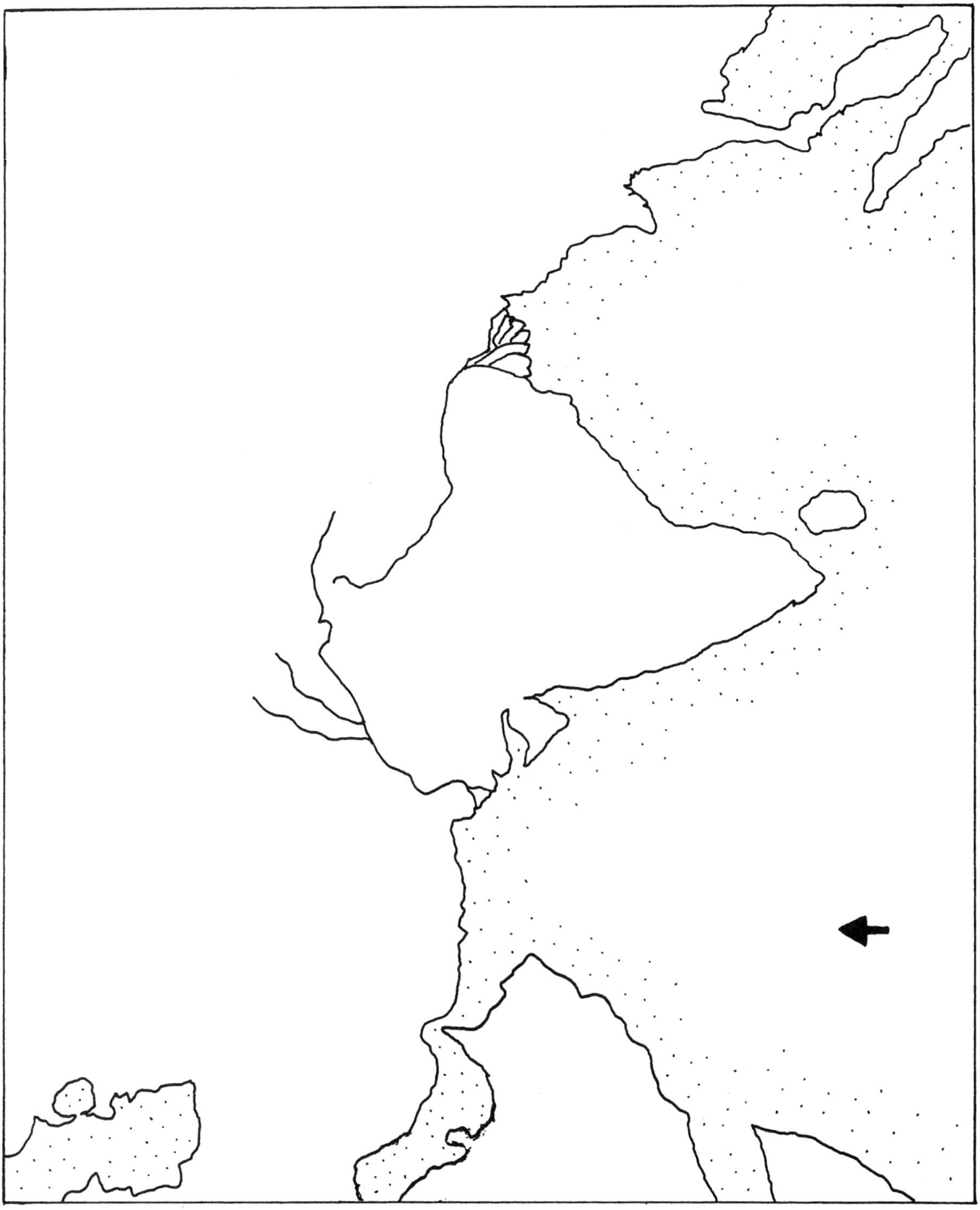

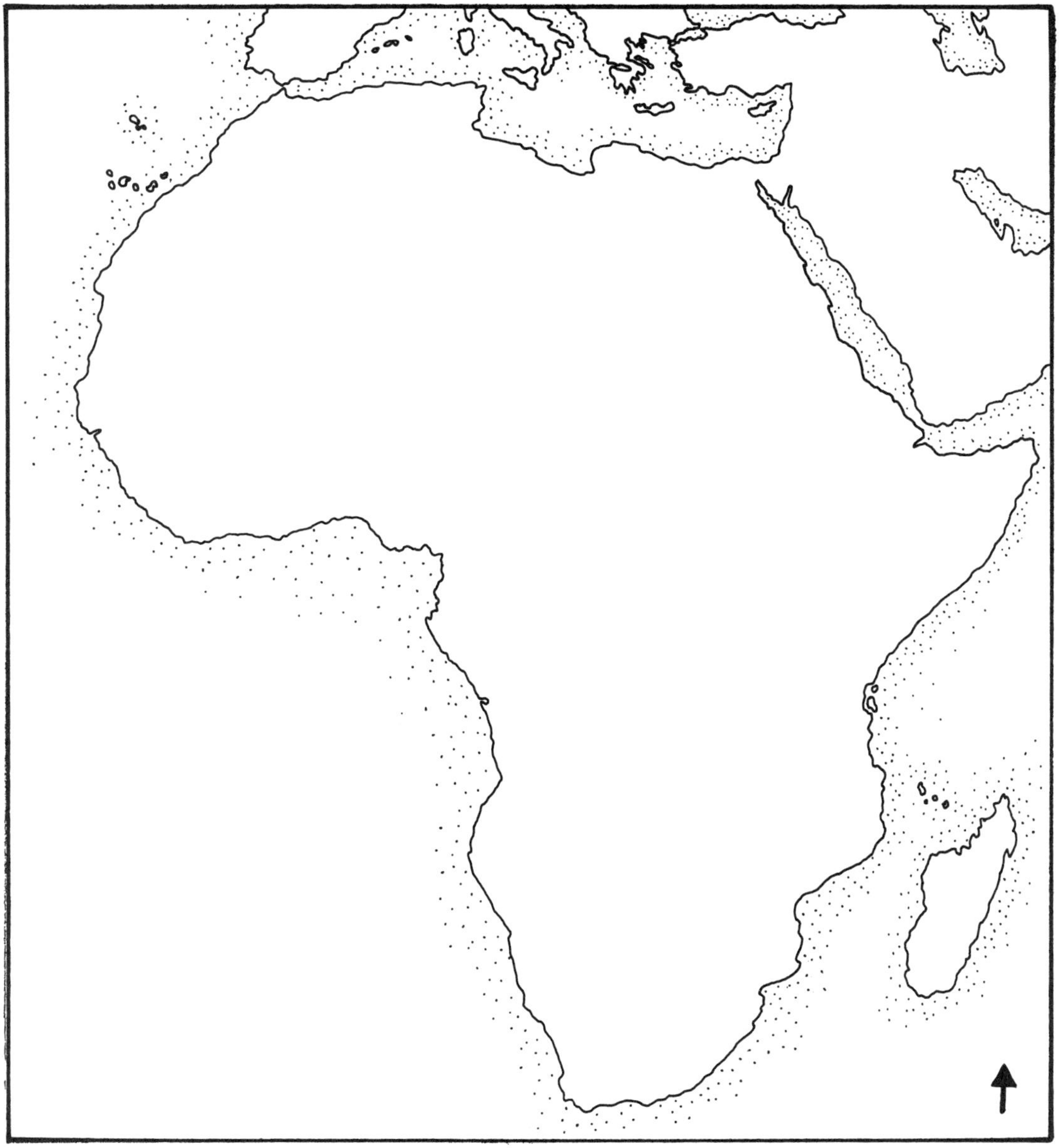